TABLE OF CONTENTS

CHAPTER 1: THE RISE OF PLASTIC

For many of us who were born after World War II, it's hard to imagine life without plastic. The use of plastics is so entrenched in our daily lives that it would take a Herculean effort to completely give it up. But at the same time, we can't turn a blind eye to the devastating effects of plastic pollution.

The amount of plastic waste produced every year is staggering. It is estimated that 8 million metric tons of plastic leak into the ocean each year. This is in addition to the 150 million metric tons that are in circulation in our vast marine environments.

It's beyond shocking that in just a matter of a few decades after mass-produced plastic was introduced to the world in 1907, the human plastic footprint now spans more than 1.6 million square kilometers of the world's oceans.

If you can't wrap your head around that figure, just think of a massive collection of plastic waste that is twice the size of Texas or three times the size of France—and still growing at an unprecedented rate year after year.

This phenomenon is known as the **Great Pacific Garbage Patch** and it is the face of the planet's plastic pollution. Discovered by Captain Charles Moore in 1997, the garbage patch is a daunting reminder of just how much damage our obsession with disposable plastics is doing to the planet.

All the plastics that we mindlessly throw in the bin don't just go away and magically disappear. They accumulate even in the most remote corners of the planet, from the Arctic to the deepest parts of the ocean—creating a **Plastic Soup**!

PLASTIC SOUP

Plastic soup is a term used to describe the large amounts of plastic waste that have accumulated in the world's oceans. Plastic debris can come from a variety of sources, including consumer products, fishing gear, and shipwrecks.

The soup is thought to be composed of tiny pieces of plastic less than 5 mm in size. These pieces are often mistaken for food by marine animals, which can lead to health complications and death. It is estimated that there are currently more than 150 million tons of plastic in the world's oceans, and that number is expected to double by 2025.

The ocean's currents help to spread the plastic soup around the world, and it is now present in every major ocean basin. The soup is particularly prevalent near coastlines and in areas where ocean currents converge. It threatens marine life and human health, and it is increasingly becoming a global environmental crisis.

There are many contributing factors to the creation of plastic soup, but the most significant one is the careless disposal of plastic waste. Plastic does not biodegrade and therefore accumulates in landfills and eventually makes its way into our oceans—harming animals, disrupting ecosystems, clogging waterways, polluting our air and water, and even entering our food chain.

Plastic waste causes serious environmental harm, including the death of aquatic animals, destruction of coral reefs, and contamination of food chains. What not many people realize is that disposable plastics also have a detrimental impact on human health. Plastic particles can enter the food chain and end up in our bodies, where they can cause cancer, reproductive problems, neurological disorders, and other health problems.

The way things are going, the human plastic footprint will continue to rise as the world becomes increasingly reliant on disposable plastics. The negative consequences of plastic pollution will only become more apparent if we don't rectify our actions.

It is now estimated that there are over 5 trillion pieces of plastic in the ocean, and it is predicted that by 2050 there will be more plastic in the ocean than fish. It's unthinkable now, but it's not a farfetched conclusion.

PLASTIC FANTASTIC!

Has plastic always been the villain that we now paint it to be?

The truth is plastic wasn't always considered a bad thing. In fact, it was once touted as a miracle material. It was lightweight, durable, and could be molded into almost any shape. It's every inventor's dream come true.

In the modern world, plastic is used in so many products that it is hard to name a consumer product that has no plastic component in it. Since the invention of plastic more than a century ago, scientists have developed many different types of plastic.

Petroleum-based plastics are the most common type, and they are made from fossil fuels. These plastics are durable and versatile. As new technology emerges, the versatility of plastic is put to good use.

Plastic has quickly replaced some traditional raw materials used in many products, such as metal, steel, and wood, in everything from cars to appliances to packaging. For example, airplane parts used to be made from metal, but now they are often made from plastic because it is lighter and cheaper.

In the early days of plastic, it was not viewed as a pollutant. There was not a huge demand for it yet, so it was not as big of a threat. However, as the years went on, the demand for plastic soared beyond expectations. The fascination with plastics turned into a dangerous obsession.

The over-reliance on plastic has created a widespread environmental crisis around the world. What was once touted as a miracle material has turned into a monster that leaves a wake of destruction wherever it goes.

Plastic is now one of the biggest pollutants in the world. Before we can thwart the plastic monster that we've created, we must first understand the essence of its existence and the reasons that make plastic a clear and present danger to our health and environment.

THE PLASTIC REVOLUTION: A TIMELINE

1856 -1870s Parkesine

Plastic was not discovered until 1856, when Alexander Parkes introduced "Parkesine," the world's first-ever man-made plastic. The new material was made from cellulose nitrate and camphor, and it could be molded into a variety of shapes.

Parkesine was very popular in the 1860s and 1870s as a substitute for ivory and was used in jewelry, buttons, brush handles, fountain pens, and billiard balls. However, because of its limitations, it was eventually replaced by a more chemically stable and more durable type of plastic.

1907 - Bakelite

The first synthetic plastic, Bakelite, was created by Leo Baekeland in 1907. He was trying to find a replacement for shellac, which was used to make electrical insulation. Bakelite is a thermoset plastic, which means that it hardens when it is heated and can't be melted again.

Bakelite is made from phenol and formaldehyde, which are two chemicals that were readily available at the time. This early plastic was virtually indestructible that it was used for a variety of items, including radios, telephones, and kitchenware.

Because Bakelite is heat resistant and non-conductive, it became a popular material for electrical components and insulation. Unlike the highly combustible nature of its predecessors, Bakelite was the first plastic that could be mass-produced because it was cheap, stable, and durable.

With its great commercial success, Bakelite marked the beginning of the modern plastics industry. It spurred research and development of other types of plastics for a variety of purposes.

1920s - Rayon and Cellophane

When rayon was developed, it gave us a soft, lightweight, and absorbent material, making it an ideal fabric for clothing. Although rayon is often mistaken for silk or cotton, it is actually made of plastic. About 80 percent of clothing sold in the United States in the 1930s contained some rayon.

When Swiss engineer JE Brandenberger found a way to roll rayon into clear viscose sheets, cellophane was born. But it was DuPont that made cellophane into a household name when it snapped up the patent and launched the flexible and moisture-proof packaging material.

Cellophane was initially used to wrap cigars, cigarettes, chocolates, and baked goods, but its potential was quickly recognized and it began to be used for a variety of other products. As cellophane can easily be molded into any shape, it became an ideal material for packaging products that need to be protected from moisture and dirt.

1926 - Polyvinyl Chloride (PVC)

Clearly, plastic is a gift that keeps on giving. With the invention of polyvinyl chloride or PVC in 1926, plastic cemented its importance to various industries—including the military. During World War II, the supply of natural rubber was dwindling, but PVC filled the void and was used to make fuel tanks, aircraft parts, and other military supplies.

Today, PVC is used in a variety of ways, including construction, piping, and other industrial applications. In construction, PVC is often used as a pipe for water or wastewater. It is also used as a sheathing material for electrical wiring. In the industrial setting, PVC is often used as a component in conveyor belts, hoses, and tubing.

PVC is also widely used in packaging food products. Because it's strong and durable, it's used for products that need to be protected during shipping, making it an ideal material for packaging items that may be subject to rough handling.

1930-1945 - Polyethylene and Nylon

In the 1930s, polyethylene (also known as polythene) was developed as a lightweight plastic that could be molded into different shapes. This versatile material quickly replaced traditional materials like metal and wood in a variety of applications.

Polyethylene is hands down the most common plastic in the world and used for practically anything you can think of like soda bottles, nylon bristle toothbrush, milk jugs, grocery bags, plastic wraps, and food storage containers, among others.

It's inexpensive, tough, and flexible. Moreover, polyethylene is considered a benign plastic, which makes it safe for use in contact with food.

1949 - Tupperware

Plastic became even more popular during peacetime. The plastic obsession was at an all-time high with the explosion in plastic consumer goods. Tupperware parties were all the rage and Tupperware became the household storage container of choice.

After World War II ended, the United States needed a way to rebuild the country. The war had left factories destroyed, homes burned down, and people homeless. Plastic seemed like the perfect solution. It was cheap to produce and could be made into just about anything.

Plastic quickly became a staple in the American economy. It was used to make everything from cars to cans of soda. And it wasn't just America that was using plastic. Countries all over the world were using it to rebuild their economies.

1950-1960 Auto Parts and Household Products

Plastic mania was strong in this period. Plastic use skyrocketed globally, with the auto-industry joining the plastic frenzy. In 1955, General Motors unveiled the Corvette, the first mass-produced American car with a fiberglass body. This new material was cheaper and lighter than metal, so it allowed for more creative designs. Plastic became the go-to material for everything from dashboards to car seats.

Many inventions and creations in the 1950s-1960s had plastic materials in them. There were two main reasons for this: 1) the development of new plastics that could be used in a wide range of applications, and 2) the rise in popularity of mass production.

From textiles to toys, to fashion and household products, plastic is practically everywhere. Lego, Barbie, Velcro, Pampers disposable diapers, plastic raincoats, PVC pipes, polyethylene bags, polystyrene foams, plastic cups, polyethylene bottles, and Kevlar are just some of the notable inventions in the years spanning 1950-1965.

1970-1980 High-Tech Gadgets and Super Fibers

Plastic continued its rise in the 1980s and reached fever-pitch with the invention of high-tech gadgets. Most, if not all, technologies in this decade were made with plastic parts. It's no wonder that in 1980 alone, 60 million metric tons of plastic were produced worldwide.

- Walkman
- Video Cassette Recorder (VCR)
- Video Game Consoles
- Answering machines
- Mobile phones
- Camcorders
- Fax machines
- Personal computers

Sharing the plastic spotlight is the further development of super fabrics. These fabrics are materials that have been designed specifically for use in wearable technology and other applications requiring high performance.

Many super fabrics are made from plastic, which makes them lightweight, durable, and moisture-wicking. They can also be treated with special coatings to protect against UV radiation.

Super fabrics are often used in sportswear, military apparel, and travel gear. Some of the latest advancements in super fabric technology include fabrics that can change color or emit light.

The best examples of super fabrics are polar fleece and Gore-Tex. Polar fleece is a synthetic fiber made from shredded plastic bottles. It is soft, stretchy, and lightweight. It keeps you warm in cold weather. It is machine-washable and does not shrink or fade.

Gore-Tex, on the other hand, is a waterproof fabric made of Teflon, a synthetic polymer. This makes Gore-Tex an ideal material for outdoor clothing and gear, as it keeps you dry while allowing your body to breathe. In addition to its waterproof properties, Gore-Tex is also windproof and highly durable. It has been used in a variety of products, including jackets, boots, backpacks, and tents.

2000 to Present - Biodegradable Plastics

Biodegradable plastics are made from renewable resources and can be broken down by bacteria or other organisms. This process of degradation returns the plastic to its natural elements, such as carbon dioxide, water, and biomass.

Many people believe that biodegradable plastics are better for the environment than traditional plastics because they do not produce harmful waste. However, there is some debate about whether or not biodegradable plastics are really better for the planet. One concern is that if these plastics are not properly disposed of, they could still release toxic chemicals.

Biodegradable plastic bags are made from plant-based materials, such as corn starch, sugar cane, wheat, sugar beets, or potatoes. Unlike traditional plastic bags, these bags can be broken down by bacteria and other organisms. This process happens naturally in soil and water, which helps reduce the amount of waste in landfills.

Bioplastic production is still in its early stages but there are now two types of bioplastics that are produced in large quantities: **Polylactic acid (PLA)** and **Polyhydroxyalkanoate (PHA)**.

PLA is made from the sugar in corn starch or sugar cane. It has the same characteristics as plastics, particularly that of polypropylene, polyethylene, or polystyrene. The difference is that PLA is biodegradable.

It can be molded into many different shapes and sizes and is often used to make biodegradable cups, containers, bottles, shrink wrap, food packaging, and medical devices (surgical pins, screws, and rods, etc.).

PHA, on the other hand, is a polymer naturally produced by bacteria through microorganism fermentation (e.g., sugar in molasses). It's not only biodegradable, but it's also biocompatible, meaning it is safe for use in contact with human tissue. PHA is used to make food packaging, implant materials, and various medical applications.

However, PHA cannot compete with traditional petroleum-based plastic because its production cost is higher. Despite this, biodegradable plastics offer a promising solution to the global problem of plastic pollution. They can help reduce our reliance on traditional plastics.

CAN WE TRUST BIOPLASTICS?

Bioplastics are derived from sustainable sources that do not rely on fossil fuels, such as vegetable fats and oils, corn, sugar cane, feathers, wood, and algae, among others. They can also be made from farming and food production leftovers that might otherwise be discarded or used for other purposes.

Common plastics are made from petroleum, which is a non-renewable resource that can take centuries to form. The process of making traditional plastics also creates toxic emissions and greenhouse gases, such as carbon dioxide.

Bioplastics are made from plant-based materials, so they are biodegradable and sustainable. They can be used to make products such as bags, cups, straws, packaging, and more. They are already being used in some countries, and their popularity is growing. As awareness of the benefits of bioplastics grows, it is likely that they will become more common in the future.

ENVIRONMENTAL IMPACT OF BIOPLASTICS

It's undeniable that bioplastics are viable alternatives to conventional petroleum-based plastics. However, bioplastics may actually be problematic because they are not as environmentally friendly as people think. Although they are made from plant-based materials, which are renewable and biodegradable, they are not necessarily 100% eco-friendly. In fact, most bioplastics require high temperatures to break down. With all the greenhouse gas emissions from processing and production, bioplastics—in reality—significantly contribute to ozone depletion and global warming.

Not many cities have the infrastructure and facilities to efficiently process bioplastics. So, they often end up in landfills where they release methane, a powerful greenhouse gas that is significantly more potent than carbon dioxide.

Aside from greenhouse emissions, bioplastics bring the problem of land use change to the fore. This is because bioplastics production requires the repurposing of land. For instance, instead of using the land for planting and harvesting corn to fulfill food requirements, it's used to produce bioplastics and biofuels. When agricultural lands are repurposed, it affects food prices and local economy.

The presence of bioplastics in the recycling stream can also cause problems for processors and recyclers. For example, the machinery used to recycle plastic can become clogged if it encounters too much biomass. In addition, there's a risk of contaminating recycled plastics.

What's more, the production of bioplastics can actually use more energy and resources than traditional plastics manufacturing, making it more costly. So, while they may be better for the environment in the long run when proper infrastructure is available, they're not necessarily better for the planet right now. It's important to weigh the shortcomings of bioplastics against the environmental effects of conventional plastics to determine if new-generation bioplastics are indeed beneficial to the environment and the planet.

PLASTIC MILESTONES THROUGH THE YEARS

NYLON BRISTLE TOOTHBRUSH

In 1937, Wallace H. Carothers, at DuPont de Nemours, developed polyamide 6.6, better known as nylon. Used a year later to replace boar hairs, this synthetic fiber marked a turning point in the history of toothbrushes.

PVC FLOORING

In 1949, manufacturing company Gerland used PVC for the first time to make a floor covering.

DISPOSABLE DIAPER

Designed in the 1950s by Procter & Gamble, the plastic disposable diaper went on sale 10 years later.

UPRIGHT VACUUM CLEANER

The first upright vacuum cleaner manufactured entirely from nylon was sold by Moulinex in 1961.

PLASTIC BOTTLE

In 1968, Vittel took the revolutionary step of producing its first plastic bottle. It weighed 36 g compared with 300 g for a glass bottle and contained 1.5 liters of water.

BANK CARD

Traditional bank cards were revolutionized by the arrival of the microchip invented by Roland Moreno. This small PVC or polypropylene card was to become an essential payment method.

DISPOSABLE RAZOR

After the Bic® ballpoint pen, in 1975, Marcel Bich invented the disposable plastic razor. Several million of these are still sold every day throughout the world.

Source: Philippe Chalmin, « The history of plastics: from the Capitol to the Tarpeian Rock », *Field Actions Science Reports* [Online], Special Issue 19 | 2019, Online since 01 March 2019, connection on 09 May 2022. URL: http://journals.openedition.org/factsreports/5071

THE WORRYING SHIFT TO SINGLE-USE PLASTICS

Plastic is often demonized for its negative environmental impact, but the reality is that not all plastics are bad. In fact, many plastics are essential to modern life and have a wide range of beneficial applications. The problem is that most of the plastic we use is single-use plastic, which is causing serious damage to our environment and our health.

Single-use plastics are those that are used once and then discarded, such as plastic straws, utensils, and packaging. These items account for a large percentage of the plastic we produce and use, and they often end up in our oceans and contribute to the growing plastic soup problem!

PLASTIC CULPRITS

Polyethylene terephthalate (PET)
PET is used to make water bottles, dispensing containers, and biscuit trays. It is a lightweight, shatter-resistant material that is also easy to recycle. In fact, water bottles made of PET can be recycled into new water bottles. While disposable water bottles are convenient, they can take hundreds of years to decompose.

High-density polyethylene (HDPE)

HDPE is a versatile plastic that can be used for a variety of purposes. It is strong and durable, making it perfect for products that need to be tough and long-lasting. Some common applications include shampoo bottles, milk bottles, ice cream containers, and freezer bags. HDPE is also resistant to chemicals and corrosion, making it ideal for use in harsh environments. Additionally, it is recyclable, making it a more sustainable choice than some other plastics.

Low-density polyethylene (LDPE)

LDPE is a type of plastic often used in single-use items such as grocery bags, cling wraps, sandwich bags, and produce bags. It is also used in bottle caps and food storage containers. LDPE is less dense than other types of plastic, which makes it less brittle and more flexible than other types of plastic. LDPE is also less likely to warp or crack when exposed to heat or sunlight.

Polypropylene (PP)

Polypropylene is a plastic made from fossil fuels. It is often used to make single-use items such as potato chip bags, microwave dishes, face masks, and bottle caps. Polypropylene is not biodegradable, meaning it does not break down in a landfill and can take centuries to decompose. When it's incinerated, it releases pollutants into the air.

Polystyrene (PS)

Polystyrene is a type of plastic that is commonly used in single-use items, such as disposable cups, plates, and cutlery. Polystyrene is made from petroleum and it is not biodegradable. When polystyrene is incinerated, it releases toxins into the air.

Expanded Polystyrene (EPS)

Expanded Polystyrene is used in making packaging materials, such as Styrofoam peanuts, hot drink cups, and other protective packaging.

MICROPLASTICS

The convenience of single-use plastic products has contributed to a throw-away society where disposable items are often used once and then tossed away. This mentality has had a devastating impact on the environment, as plastic products can take centuries to decompose. In addition, many plastic items are not recyclable, which means they eventually end up in landfills and oceans.

About 36 percent of all plastics produced today are used in packaging such as food and beverage containers. Plastic straws, bags, cups, and utensils are the most commonly used plastic products that are thrown away after a single short use—and 85 percent of them end up in landfills!

As plastics are not biodegradable, they often end up staying in landfills for long periods of time. The longer plastic stays in a landfill, the more likely it is to break down into smaller and smaller pieces called microplastics.

Microplastics, defined as plastic particles less than 5 mm in size, are a pervasive form of pollution found in land, sea, and air.

When plastics are found even in the air we breathe, the water we drink, and the food we eat, then we know that plastic pollution has reached critical levels.

What's worrying is that microplastics have been found in virtually every corner of the globe. In fact, microfiber fallout in a suburb of Paris and in the Chinese city of Dongguan were measured. It was recorded that between 2 and 355 microfibers per square meter per day were counted in the Paris suburb, while in Dogguan, 175 to 313 microplastics per square meter were counted. Most of the microplastics found were of synthetic microfiber origin.

The findings revealed that microplastics are not just in the oceans or outdoor air; they are, in fact, also inside our homes, offices, and pretty much every indoor location.

Microplastics could come from a variety of sources, such as clothing, tires, or construction materials. Among these culprits, textile fibers are the leading source of microplastics in the air and indoors.

A large contributor to this form of pollution is synthetic clothing, which can release millions of microfibers each time it's washed. These fibers are too small to be captured by wastewater treatment plants, meaning they end up in the environment where they can harm aquatic life and enter the food chain.

Out of the total plastic production in the world, about 16 percent is textile fibers. Microfibers from clothing made with synthetic materials are the largest contributor to microplastic pollution. Since microplastics are in the clothes we wear, they can be inhaled or ingested without us knowing it!

With 33 percent of the indoor fibers coming from plastic, it's safe to conclude that we're likely to ingest household microfibers from clothing than from eating fish and seafood.

What does this all mean to our health?

Since it has already been established that synthetic fibers and microplastic are present in both outdoor and indoor air, this should raise concerns about the potential risks associated with exposure.

Microfibers are particularly concerning because they are so small that they can be inhaled. They can also attract other pollutants like heavy metals, which may increase the risk of health complications. Studies have shown that exposure to microplastics can cause harm to aquatic animals, and there is growing evidence that they may also be detrimental to humans.

Scientists have a reason to believe that microplastics may contribute to the risk of lung cancer when microplastics were found in human lung tissue. If the level of microplastic inhalation is considerably high, it can cause inflammation, trigger asthma attacks, or cause cancer.

More research is needed to determine the full extent of the health risks associated with breathing in plastic fibers and microplastics, but if current research findings are any indication, plastic pollution is not just an environmental issue but a health issue as well.

MICROBEADS AND LIQUID MICROPLASTICS

Microbeads are tiny pieces of plastic found in cosmetics, body washes, lotions, shampoos, toothpaste, and soap. They're less than five millimeters wide and are often used as an abrasive to help exfoliate skin.

The popularity of microbeads has led to concerns about their impact on the environment. It is estimated that 8 trillion microbeads are released into U.S. waterways each day. That's enough to cover 300 tennis courts every day.

Microbeads can have adverse effects to fish because they look like food. The beads can also absorb toxins, which can be passed along to the animals that eat them.

A fairly new pollutant that's just as notorious as microbeads are liquid microplastics in cosmetics. These are poorly biodegradable synthetic polymers used in hair styling products and sunblocks. They're hard to detect and thus earned the moniker, "hidden plastics" No matter what they are called, they have the same devastating effects as microbeads.

PLASTIC ADDITIVES

Additives are important to the manufacture of plastic materials because they help improve the physical and chemical properties of the end product. They can enhance the plastic's color, strength, durability, and other properties. Additives can also help protect against ultraviolet radiation and oxidation.

Some additives act as plasticizers, which make the material more flexible. Others work as flame retardants, stabilizers, or antioxidants to improve the toughness or durability of the plastic. In some cases, coloring agents or other additives may be included to change the appearance or performance of the finished product.

There are a wide variety of different additives that can be used in plastics, and each one has its own set of benefits and drawbacks. Some additives can have a damaging effect to human health or the environment, so it is important to understand what each one does before using them.

BPA

Bisphenol A (BPA) is an industrial chemical that has been used since the 1950s to make certain plastics and resins. BPA is found in many common consumer products, including water bottles, food storage containers, and dental sealants.

The use of BPA has come under scrutiny in recent years because some research suggests that it may have negative effects to human health. Studies have shown that BPA can interfere with the normal functioning of the endocrine system, and may increase the risk of certain diseases, including cancer and heart disease.

A growing number of consumer products now come labeled with a "BPA-free" designation, but it is not clear how safe these alternatives are. More research is needed to determine the health risks posed by BPA and other chemicals that interact with the endocrine system.

FLAME RETARDANTS

Flame retardants are chemicals that are added to plastics in order to make them more resistant to catching on fire. They are often necessary to meet regulatory and governmental standards so that the plastic will not combust.

Call them necessary evils because these chemicals have been linked to a variety of health problems, including cancer.

One of the biggest concerns with flame retardants is their ability to accumulate in the environment. This means that they can end up in the food chain, where they can potentially cause harm to both humans and wildlife due to their toxicity.

Another issue is that when you recycle plastic products, the flame retardants remain in the plastic. That's because flame retardants cannot be removed from plastics through the recycling process.

However, There are a few things you can do to reduce your exposure to flame retardants. You can avoid eating foods that have been packaged in plastic, and you can try to avoid using plastic for food preparation and storage. You can also avoid using household cleaners that come in plastic containers.

FISHING NETS, ROPES, AND LINES

One of the most common forms of marine litter are fishing nets, ropes, and traps. Nets can be made of different materials, but most are made of plastic. They can be very large and often get tangled up in coral reefs and other marine habitats.

They also contribute to the growing problem of plastic pollution. As they break down, they release tiny pieces of plastic that can be ingested by fish and other aquatic species. This type of pollution is a major threat to marine ecosystems.

Fishing nets are often lost or abandoned at sea. Abandoned or lost fishing gear known as "ghost nets" accounts for about 46 percent of all marine debris. Ghost nets can drift for years, ensnaring sea turtles, dolphins, and other creatures.

These ghost nets can take centuries to decompose. As a result, they frequently end up trapping and killing ocean plants and animals. The problem with fishing nets is that they are often made of plastic, which does not biodegrade. This means that even if a net is abandoned at sea, it will still be there years later, silently killing inhabitants.

One of the biggest problems with abandoned fishing nets is that they can trap marine animals. This can lead to them being suffocated or injured. In addition, the nets can also damage coral reefs and other underwater habitats.

When the plastic breaks down into small pieces, it can pollute the water and make it difficult for fish to thrive. In addition to posing a danger to wildlife, discarded nets also contribute to the growing problem of microplastic pollution.

Why should we care about plastic fishing nets and ropes?

Fishing nets, ropes, and lines made of plastic can be mistaken for food by marine animals at all levels of the food chain, including fish, seabirds, sea turtles, and dolphins. This can lead to death by starvation, choking, or strangulation. Ingestion of plastic particles can cause health problems for small fish, including digestive blockages and toxicity.

The larger fish that eat these smaller fish can also accumulate high levels of microplastics in their tissues, leading to potential health risks for humans who eat them. We are at risk of consuming fish contaminated with toxic plastic particles.

Plastic is made from petroleum, so when it photodegrades (breaks down from exposure to light), it releases toxins like bisphenol-A (BPA) and polychlorinated biphenyls (PCBs). These toxins can be ingested by fish, which can then be eaten by other animals up the food chain. These toxins are known as endocrine disruptors, meaning they interfere with the hormones in our bodies. They can cause reproductive problems, developmental delays, and even cancer.

This is clear evidence that plastic has already infiltrated the food chain, posing a serious threat to both human health and the environment. It underscores the need for better waste management practices and for reducing our reliance on disposable plastics.

What's particularly frustrating is that governments are not finding a real solution to address the problem of ghost nets. These abandoned fishing nets can drift for years, ensnaring sea turtles, dolphins, and other creatures.

But because there's no system in place to identify which ship the ghost nets came from, no one is willing to shoulder the clean-up cost. Governments abandon the problem just as irresponsible fish folks dump and abandon fish nets in the ocean.

CHAPTER 2: DROWNING IN PLASTIC

In recent decades, the production of plastic packaging has increased dramatically. This is largely due to the advantages that plastic has over other materials. Plastic is lightweight, durable, and moisture-resistant, which makes it an ideal material for packaging. As a result, the use of plastic packaging has become increasingly common in a variety of industries, including food and beverage, cosmetics, and pharmaceuticals.

Plastic production and disposal come with a high environmental cost. The demand for plastic packaging is constantly increasing as the world population grows and becomes more affluent.

Despite the growing concern over plastic pollution, the production of plastics is estimated to increase exponentially in the next few years and there are no signs of slowing down. However, with inadequate facilities and the inability to sustainably manage plastic waste, our world is in for a rude awakening.

In addition to the environmental impact, plastic production also has human health implications. Plastic can contain noxious chemicals that can leach into food and water supplies. These chemicals can cause health problems such as cancer and infertility.

While some countries are beginning to restrict or ban disposable plastics, most have yet to take any significant action. Unless there is a major shift in consumer behavior, it's likely that plastic production will continue to grow at an alarming rate.

THE CURRENT STATE OF PLASTIC PRODUCTION

Since the 1950s, when plastic was first mass-produced, humans have created 8.3 billion metric tons of plastic materials in different shapes, sizes, and functions. For perspective, that's the weight of one million blue whales.

The amount of plastic produced each year has substantially increased from 1.5 million metric tons in 1950 to 380 million metric tons in 2021.

A large majority of this plastic is used for packaging and disposable items, which are often discarded after a single use.

The global plastic production is estimated to have decreased by 0.3 percent in 2020, compared with 2019, according to a report released by Statista. This downturn was largely attributed to the impact of the COVID-19 pandemic on the plastics industry.

Europe and North America were the regions that saw the biggest decline in plastic production, due to factory shutdowns and plummeting demand from consumers. In contrast, Asia Pacific – which has been one of the fastest-growing regions for plastic production in recent years – recorded only a modest slowdown in 2020.

Despite this overall decline in 2020, there are still some segments of the plastics industry that are performing relatively well. For instance, demand for high-value applications such as medical devices and automotive parts has remained strong.

The plastics industry projects that over the next decade, demand for plastics will grow further. It's attributing its future growth to the increasing global population and demands for more plastic consumer goods. This growth is being driven by increased consumption in developing countries, the increasing buying power of the middle class, and a rising demand for lightweight, durable materials in automotive and electronics applications.

However, this burgeoning demand for plastic also comes with a cost. Plastic pollution has become a major environmental issue. To combat this problem, the industry needs to invest in new technologies and practices that will minimize waste and promote recycling efforts.

PLASTIC PRODUCTION BY REGION

Where are the plastics coming from? The level of plastic production in each region is largely determined by the level of economic development and the use of plastics in various industries.

For example, Asia-Pacific has a large population and a growing economy, which has led to increased demand for plastics in packaging and consumer products. North America has a high concentration of plastics manufacturers, fulfilling demands from various industries around the world.

CHINA

For a number of years, China has been the world's leading producer of plastic materials, accounting for 32 percent of global production in 2020. This makes China the largest exporter of plastic materials.

The country has seen rapid growth in plastics production in recent years, as it seeks to meet rising demand from domestic and international markets. This growth has come at a cost to the environment, as China's plastics industry is heavily reliant on fossil fuels and produces large amounts of pollution.

China is expected to produce more of the world's plastic in the coming years. This is largely due to the country's growing middle class, which has led to an increase in demand for products made with plastic.

China is not only the largest producer of plastic in the world, but it is also one of the biggest consumers. The country has been working to reduce its dependence on imported oil, and plastics are seen as a way to achieve this goal. As a result, Chinese companies are investing in new technologies that will allow them to produce more plastic domestically to promote economic growth.

The growth of the Chinese plastics industry has had a ripple effect throughout the world. Many other countries are now looking to increase their own production capacity, in order to meet rising demand.

NAFTA COUNTRIES

The North American Free Trade Agreement (NAFTA) went into effect on January 1, 1994. The trade bloc includes the United States, Canada and Mexico. NAFTA eliminated most tariffs on goods traded among the member countries.

Collectively, NAFTA countries contributed 19 percent share of the total plastic production in the world. This made NAFTA the second-largest producing region

Trade blocs like NAFTA are designed to promote free trade among member countries. By eliminating tariffs on goods traded among member countries, businesses in those countries can compete more fairly. This leads to lower prices for consumers and increased competition, which can spur innovation and economic growth.

JAPAN AND THE REST OF ASIA

Collectively, Asia accounts for more than half of the 367 million tons of global plastics production in 2020. Japan's 3 percent share is a distant second to China's 32 percent, while the rest of Asia produces 17 percent of the world's plastics.

Malaysia has been rapidly increasing its production of plastic and Thailand is also seeing a dramatic increase in plastic production. These countries are largely producing cheap plastics for export to other countries in Asia and around the world. This increase in plastic production is having serious consequences, including creating massive amounts of waste and polluting waterways.

EUROPE

Europe has a long and established history in plastics production. In 2020, Europe produced 55 million metric tons of plastic, which is equivalent to 15 percent of the total global production. This is a decrease of 5 percent compared to the 2019 figure. This is attributed to the decrease in demand as a result of a decline in the production packaging and automotive sectors, which heavily use plastics. The pandemic also had a hand in the decline because the industry streamlined its

MIDDLE EAST AND AFRICA

Plastics production in the Middle East and Africa accounts for 7% of total global production in 2020. This is due to the growth of the plastics industry in these regions, which is forecasted to continue at a rapid pace. In particular, Saudi Arabia and South Africa are expected to be among the top countries in terms of plastics production. The increasing local and international demand for plastics is driving the growth of the industry in these regions.

LATIN AMERICA

In recent years, the Latin American plastics industry has seen significant growth. In 2020, Latin America's plastics production account for 4 percent of the total world production. This can be attributed to a number of factors, including the rise in disposable income and population growth in the region. Brazil is the second largest producer of plastics in Latin America, next to Mexico.

The plastics industry is a vital part of the Latin American economy, and it is projected to continue growing in the years ahead. Plastics are used in a wide variety of products, from automotive parts to packaging materials. Manufacturers in Latin America are capitalizing on this growing demand and are investing in new production facilities to meet the needs of consumers.

The industry faces some challenges, including rising labor costs and access to raw materials. However, with continued investment and innovation, the Latin American plastics industry is poised for continued growth in the years ahead.

COMMONWEALTH OF INDEPENDENT STATES (CIS)

The CIS is a major producer of plastics, which accounts for 3% of the total word plastics production. In 2017, the CIS produced over 9 million metric tons of plastics, with Russia as the largest producer with over 4 million metric tons of plastics produced.

The Commonwealth of Independent States (CIS) is a regional organization that was established in 1991. The purpose of the CIS is to promote cooperation between the member states. The CIS has 9 member states: Armenia, Azerbaijan, Belarus, Georgia, Kazakhstan, Kyrgyzstan, Moldova, Russia, and Tajikistan.

THE BIGGEST POLLUTERS

The world's oceans are choking on plastic. When plastic waste isn't properly disposed of, it often ends up in our oceans. It is estimated that 8 million metric tons of plastic enter our oceans every year. That's equivalent to a garbage truck full of plastic dumped into our seas every minute.

China and the United States are among the biggest contributors to plastic pollution. China is the world's leading producer of plastic packaging, while the United States is the top consumer.

Plastic is polluting the world's oceans at an alarming rate and here are the biggest polluters based on their estimated contribution to plastic pollution in million tons of plastic waste.

1. China (59 million tons)
2. United States (38 million tons)
3. Germany (14 million tons)
4. Brazil (12 million tons)
5. Japan (8 million tons)
6. Pakistan (6 million tons)
7. Nigeria (6 million tons)
8. Russia (6 million tons)
9. Turkey (5 million tons)
10. Egypt (5 million tons)

The amount of plastic in our oceans is predicted to triple by 2025 unless these countries take action to curb the plastic production and consumption.

SECTORS THAT USE THE MOST PLASTIC IN THE WORLD

The global production of plastics is allocated to a range of industries, sectors, and product uses. Automotive, construction, textile, packaging, electronic & electronics, transportation, industrial machinery, and consumer & industrial are some of the key sectors that use plastic products. Plastic manufacturers earmark their plastic production to these sectors.

Keep in mind that the largest consumer of plastic does not necessarily mean that they generate the most plastic waste as there are other factors at play that influence the lifetime of the end product.

The **Packaging** sector is one of the most important users of plastics and has been a key driver of demand. In particular, rigid packaging has been a mainstay of the sector, thanks to its durability and protective properties. High demand for single-use plastics also contribute to the more than 146 million tons allocated for the packaging sector. The packaging sector is the largest user of plastic resins, accounting for more than one-third of all resin consumption.

A distant second is the **Building and Construction** sector, with over 65 million tons of plastics at its disposal. It's a large consumer of plastic composites used in window and door frames, roofing materials, and insulation, among other things.

The **Textile** sector is the third largest consumer of plastics. It uses more than 59 million tons of plastic to manufacture synthetic fibres, which are used to make fabrics for clothing. Plastics can be very effective at preventing moisture loss and providing insulation, so they are often used in fabrics that need to be waterproof or thermally insulated.

The combined **Consumer and Institutional Products sector** uses more than 42 million tons of plastic for a wide range of products including furniture, toys, household products, leisure, sports equipment, office supplies, and medical supplies.

The **Transportation** sector uses more than 27 million tons of plastics in a wide range of applications, from exterior body panels to under-the-hood components.

The **Electrical and Electronics** sector uses more than 18 million tons of plastic for consumer durables, appliances, electronic components, and communication equipment. The demand for these products is increasing due to the rise in population and income levels.

The **Industrial Machinery** sector is a big user of plastics. Plastic components can be designed to be very lightweight, which can help reduce the weight of the machinery and make it more fuel efficient. In addition, plastic parts can often be molded into very complex shapes, which can help improve the performance and reliability of the machinery. Finally, plastic parts can also be made to be corrosion-resistant, which can help prolong the life of the machinery.

WHO MAKES THE MOST WASTE?

In terms of sectors, the top two biggest producers of plastic waste are **Packaging** and **Textiles**.

Here's why:

- Packaging accounts for about 40 percent of all plastic waste, a large part of which are ocean-bound trash. Most of this waste comes from single-use plastics like straws, cups, and bottles.

- The textile sector is responsible for producing large amounts of plastic waste in the form of microplastics and microfibers. It accounts for 14 percent of all plastic waste.

- The sector also produces large amounts of conventional plastic waste, which consists of packaging materials used to ship textiles around the world. A recent study found that a single garment can produce an average of 1.7 pounds of waste, most of which is not recyclable.

BIGGEST CORPORATE POLLUTERS IN THE WORLD

Plastic pollution is one of the most pressing environmental issues of our time. The world's oceans are choking in plastic waste, and all data indicates that it's only going to get worse. Despite this, many corporations continue to deny the extent of the plastic pollution problem and downplay its effects to the environment. As a result, there's lack of significant and meaningful action to address the issue.

This corporate denial is both irresponsible and dangerous. It is long past time for corporations to face up to this crisis and take steps to reduce the world's reliance on plastics and find sustainable way to move away from disposable plastics and towards reusable alternatives.

THE USUAL SUSPECTS

According to the environmental advocacy organization Break Free from Plastic, **the Coca-Cola Company, PepsiCo, Inc., and Nestlé** are among the world's biggest corporate plastic polluters for three consecutive years covering 2019, 2020, and 2021.

In an effort to identify the most common plastic polluters, global beach cleanups were carried out by more than 11,000 volunteers in 45 countries. The most commonly found items were plastic bottles, cigarette butts, and food wrappers. The findings only reflect what was found on the surface of the sand and do not account for all plastic pollution.

The top brand plastic polluters are the following:

1. Coca-Cola Company
2. PepsiCo Inc
3. Nestle S.A.
4. Unilever plc
5. Mondelez International
6. Mars Incorporated
7. Procter & Gamble (P&G)
8. Philip Morris International
9. Colgate-Palmolive Company
10. Perfetti Van Melle

Coca-Cola ranked first on the list of companies with the most plastic pollution found in waterways around the world. It has a plastic footprint of more than 2.9 million tons per year. Not far behind was PepsiCo, whose bottling plants in India were identified as a major source of plastic pollution. Nestlé has been criticized for its reliance on single-use PET bottles.

Although the top three brands found were Coca-Cola, PepsiCo., and Nestlé, many other brands were also identified. Rounding out the top 10 are Unilever, Mondelez International, Mars Incorporated, Procter & Gamble, Philip Morris International, Colgate-Palmolive, and Perfetti van Melle.

Further research is needed to determine how these brands can be held accountable for their role in marine litter. In the meantime, it is important for consumers to be aware of which companies are producing excessive amounts of waste and make choices that support sustainable practices.

FALSE SOLUTIONS

COCA-COLA'S PLEDGE: WORLD WITHOUT WASTE

In a bid to reduce its plastic pollution, Coca-Cola launched World Without Waste campaign in 2018. The goal is to make all Coke product packaging recyclable by 2023 and to use 50% recycled material in their packaging by 2030. More specifically, Coca-Cola would collect and recycle one bottle for every one sold.

With this pledge, Coke is setting an example for other major corporations to follow suit. On paper, Coke's commitment to recycling will help reduce the amount of waste that ends up in landfills and oceans. However, based on brand audits by Greenpeace Southeast Asia and Break Free From Plastic, the company has only recycled 2% of the plastic it pledged to collect. This indicates that Coca-Cola's efforts have very little impact on the wider problem of plastic pollution.

Greenpeace went so far as to say that giant corporations are investing in false solutions because the initiatives do not move us away from single-plastic use and throwaway culture. With poor results, it's clear that companies do not have the ability to follow through. What makes things worse is that Coca-Cola continues to increase its plastic waste every year, despite its promise to recycle.

PEPSICO'S PEP+

In an effort to become more sustainable, PepsiCo launched the PEP+ (PepsiCo Plus) initiative, which focuses on reducing the company's environmental impact. The goal is to achieve net-zero emissions by 2040, become net water positive, and improve packaging sustainability with the intention to reduce virgin plastic per serving by 50 percent.

More specifically, PepsiCo is looking to expand its SodaStream business to eliminate the use of more than 200 billion plastic bottles by 2030. Although PepsiCo's initiative is noble, it has failed to address one of the biggest environmental problems caused by its products, such as plastic pollution.

NESTLE'S SUSTAINABLE PACKAGING

Nestle is committed to making 100% of their **packaging recyclable or reusable by 2025** and reduce the use of virgin plastics by one-third. The company is implementing an ambitious waste-free packaging strategy involving a new recycling technology that will allow them to recycle PET bottles back into food-grade quality plastic. This is a huge step in the fight against plastic pollution, and if Nestle can achieve these goals, it will set a new standard for the food industry.

One of the main problems with recycling is that not all plastic can be recycled. Some types of plastic are downcycled into lower-quality materials, which defeats the purpose of recycling. But Nestle's new recycling technology will enable them to recycle PET bottles back into food-grade quality plastic, which can be used again for packaging.

GRADE: F FOR FAILURE

Being the top three biggest polluters, these companies are hoping to set an example for other businesses and demonstrate that sustainability is important for both the environment and the bottom line. However, there is a huge disparity between the goals of the initiatives and the results. Despite the huge investments made to curb plastic pollution, the initiatives proved to be big failures.

In the midst of the devastating plastic pollution crisis, these fast-moving consumer goods (FMCG) companies have made commitments to appear to be part of the solution. However, they are still part of the problem and the problem only keeps getting bigger.

Why so?

The argument is that these companies are seemingly doing the bare minimum to pacify the clamor for change. They do this by developing false solutions in any of these forms:

- **Diverting blame** (e.g., blaming consumers for littering)

  The consumer goods industry is facing increasing scrutiny over the amount of plastic pollution that is being produced. Manufacturers and FMCG companies are blaming consumers for the problem, but it is clear that they are not doing enough to reduce their own contributions.

- **Greenwashing existing products or processes** (e.g., claiming biodegradability when a product is still made of plastic)

  Greenwashing is the act of misleading consumers about the environmental benefits of a product or service. Some common greenwashing tactics include using vague language, making unsubstantiated claims, or overstating the product's benefits.

One of the main solutions that companies are proposing is to increase the use of biodegradable plastics. However, these materials often do not break down properly and they still contribute to the overall pollution problem. In addition, many companies are not making it clear which products are actually biodegradable. As a result, consumers may end up buying a product that actually harms the environment. Greenwashing can divert attention from real issues and solutions.

- **Delaying real change** (e.g., promoting refillables without addressing the underlying issues with disposable plastics).

Although some companies have taken steps to reduce their plastic waste, most have not made any significant changes. Many of their corporate pledges lack specific goals or timelines. As such, they are being called out for their role in contributing to plastic pollution and the failure to address the underlying issues.

One of the main problems with disposable plastics is the way they are used and disposed of. Many major companies produce products that rely on disposable plastics, but they fail to provide adequate recycling or disposal options. This creates a lot of waste that often ends up in landfills and oceans.

More stringent guidelines are needed to ensure that these corporate polluters take meaningful action to address the problem of plastic pollution. We need corporate leaders to step up and pledge real change.

GOVERNMENT'S WEAK POLICIES ON PLASTIC POLLUTION

It has become apparent that corporate commitments are nothing more than greenwashing, a cynical ploy to make it look like these companies are doing something when they are actually not doing enough. The only way to address the plastic pollution crisis is with strong legislation that prohibits single-use plastics and holds corporations accountable for their contribution to the problem.

We now know that we can't fully rely on FMCG companies to take action against plastic pollution. But what about the government?

Governments around the world have been unwilling to take serious action on the plastic pollution crisis. The problem has been growing for years, and yet most governments have done little more than establish a few token policies.

This is in part due to the complexity of the issue—plastic pollution is caused by many different factors, and it's not always clear what measures should be taken to address it. But it's also because of the vested interests of powerful industries that rely on disposable plastics. Until there is pressure from voters and consumers, governments are unlikely to take meaningful steps to address this crisis.

Does this mean fighting plastic pollution is a lost cause? Although combating plastic pollution is such an uphill battle, it doesn't mean all hope is lost.

Plastic waste pollution is a global problem that will require collaborative efforts from both international organizations and future generations to mitigate.

Despite the many challenges posed by plastic pollution, there are some promising initiatives being undertaken to address the problem. For example, the United Nations Environment Programme (UNEP) has launched a global campaign to reduce plastic waste called "Clean Seas". This campaign aims to engage governments, businesses, and individuals in reducing the amount of plastic that enters the ocean. Additionally, grassroots organizations like 5 Gyres Institute are working to raise awareness about the dangers of plastic pollution and inspire change at a local level.

The even bigger question is what is the United States government doing? This is a valid concern considering that the US is on top of the plastic waste polluter totem pole.

It's clear that Americans are catching on to the dangers of plastic pollution and are demanding change. In fact, in an Ipsos survey on attitudes towards single use plastics, 55 percent of Americans agreed that single-use plastics should be banned.

The same sentiment is shared by people from 28 other countries who participated in the survey, which covered more than 20,000 respondents under the age of 75.

This goes to show that people are starting to wake up to this issue and demand change. States and cities are beginning to ban single-use plastics, such as straws, bags, and cups and businesses are starting to phase them out too. This is a positive step in the right direction, but much more needs to be done to address this growing problem.

States have tried to address plastic pollution within their local communities, imposing bans or fees on plastic shopping bags. However, the reality is that there is no national policy to address the issue.

The United States has not ratified the Basel Convention, which would allow for better international cooperation on the management of plastic waste. Without ratification of the treaty, the United States cannot participate in decisions about how best to manage and reduce plastic pollution both domestically and internationally.

If there's a glimmer of hope, it's in the state-wide initiatives. In what could be seen as a victory for the planet, three states implemented bans on single-use plastic bags. This signals a shift in the way the US deals with environmental issues. The bans are an effort to reduce the amount of plastic waste that ends up in landfills and oceans.

California became the first state in the US to enact a state-wide ban on single-use plastic bags at large retail stores. The purpose of the bill is to reduce the use of plastic bags by imposing a 10-cent fee, encouraging people to use alternative bags, such as those made of paper or reusable fabric.

Supporters of the measure say it will help reduce litter and protect marine species, while opponents argue that it will lead to job losses and higher prices for consumers. It is estimated that California spends $25 million annually cleaning up plastic bag litter.

In **Hawaii**, all of the most populous counties prohibit non-biodegradable plastic bags at checkout, as well as paper bags with less than 40% recyclable materials. The ban went into effect between 2011 and 2015 in Kauai, Maui and Hawaii counties.

With the passage of Senate Bill 1508, **New York** became the third state to ban plastic bags in 2019. The law, which went into effect in January 2020, prohibits grocery stores, pharmacies, convenience stores, and retail shops from providing customers with single-use plastic bags. Stores will be allowed to provide paper bags but only if the customer pays a minimum five-cent fee.

This measure will reduce the amount of waste New Yorkers produce each year. According to state figures, New Yorkers discard an estimated **23 billion single-use plastic bags** annually. That's enough plastic to circle the Earth more than 550 times.

Currently, there are only eight states with **plastic bag legislation**. This barely moves the needle, but it's a good start.

- California
- Connecticut
- Delaware
- Hawaii
- Maine
- New York
- Oregon
- Vermont

Why just 8 states, you ask? The reality is that some states are pre-emptively passing laws that would prevent any such bans. This is in part a response to the lobbying of the plastics industry, which is arguing that such bans would be costly and ineffective. This explains the government's unwillingness to take drastic actions to curb the plastic pollution problem.

In 2021, there are more than 500 local plastic bag ordinances that have been adopted in 28 states. Eight states have adopted state-wide plastic bag reduction laws. This movement towards reducing the use of plastic bags is being driven by local governments because state pre-emption laws prevent them from passing more stringent regulations.

Just when we thought things couldn't get any more complicated, three new plastic pollution pre-emption laws were enacted in Ohio, Nebraska, and South Dakota, bringing the total number of nationwide pre-emption laws to 18.

These laws prohibit local governments from enacting their own restrictions on plastic bags, straws, and other disposable items. This is a major setback for the efforts to reduce plastic pollution, as local governments are often more responsive to the needs of their communities and can be more effective in tackling this issue. Environmentalists and other stakeholders are working to overturn them, but they have to jump through all sorts of hoops to battle it out with lobbyists and the establishment.

While the plastic bans are a step in the right direction, they only apply to certain municipalities or counties within each state. It will be important for these initiatives to spread to other parts of the states if they are to have a real impact.

There is also some concern that the bans will lead to job losses in the plastics industry. However, many companies are already transitioning to more sustainable materials and it is possible that new jobs will be created in the renewable energy sector.

WHAT ARE PRE-EMPTION LAWS?

Pre-empting local plastic pollution control ordinances is an effort that is playing out at the state level of government, where corporate lobbyists and conservative lawmakers are working together to strip cities and counties of their ability to pass laws that would reduce plastic pollution.

This effort is motivated by a desire to protect the profits of the plastics industry. Bypassing local governments, these lawmakers can enact state-wide policies that are friendlier to the industry and that supersede any local measures that might be more protective of the environment.

This troubling development comes as communities around the country are increasingly looking for ways to reduce plastic pollution. Plastic waste is a serious environmental problem and local governments are in a unique position to address it.

CHAPTER 3: PLASTIC HABITS

The use of plastic is a staple in our lives from the time we are born until the time we die. Babies are swaddled in plastic blankets, given plastic bottles, and bathed in water stored in plastic containers. As children, we play with colorful plastic toys, watch shows from TV with parts made entirely of plastic, and eat food that has been wrapped in it.

Even as adults, we rely on disposable, single-use plastics for our convenience. Many of us have jobs that require us to use plastic products on a daily basis. We sit on chairs made from plastic, drive cars with dashboards covered in it, and sleep on mattresses filled with synthetic materials. Plastic is so pervasive in our lives that it's hard to imagine living without it.

If you think about it, we use plastic in just about everything we do. There are the obvious items, like grocery bags and water bottles, but there are also the not-so-obvious items, like toothbrushes and contact lenses.

So how much plastic do we actually use in our lifetime?

The answer is a lot! In fact, the average person in North America or Western Europe uses around **100 kilograms (220 pounds)** of plastic each year.

In Asia, the average person uses just 20 kilograms (44 pounds), but as the countries develop and expand, it is expected that plastic use will increase rapidly and exponentially in the coming years.

With the global average life expectancy of 72.6 years, a person would have consumed 7,200 kilograms of plastic in his or her lifetime. And that translates to a lot of plastic waste!

FROM BIRTH TO ADULTHOOD

It's no secret that plastic pollution is a huge problem. In fact, it's been called the "greatest environmental challenge of our time." And while there are many sources of plastic pollution, our plastic habits are a big part of the problem.

For starters, we use way too much plastic. We use single-use plastics like straws and bags for just a few minutes before discarding them – often in landfills or waterways where they can take centuries to break down.

In addition to using too much plastic, we also recycle very little of it. In the US, for example, only about 9 percent of all plastics are recycled.

While some of that plastic can be recycled, most of it ends up in landfills or the ocean. Here's how our plastic habits are destroying the environment and killing ocean life.

Plastic baby bottles

In the United States, plastic bottles made up the largest share of the baby bottle market in 2018. This segment was valued at around $250.1 million and is expected to increase to $426.4 million in 2026. The demand for glass bottles, on the other hand, has been declining in recent years. One reason for this is that plastic bottles are cheaper to produce than glass ones. They are also shatter-resistant and can be reused multiple times.

Plastic baby bottles are typically made of polypropylene. While it's generally considered safe for use, it does not take away the fact that they're non-biodegradable. The more they accumulate, the more they become a threat to the health of humans and animals.

When plastic baby bottles are shaken, heated, and sterilized, they release microplastics which get mixed in the baby formula. This tells us that bottle-fed infants are exposed to microplastics. But how much is the exposure?

According to a study by Li, et al (2020), polypropylene infant feeding bottles (IFBs) release as much as 16.2 million microplastic particles per liter. Depending on the region, the potential exposure of babies up to 12 months old range from 14,600 to 4,550,000 particles per capita per day. This suggests that the exposure of bottle-fed infants to microplastics is higher than what was previously recognized.

The health implications of this contamination in the long term are currently unknown but warrant further study.

Disposable Diapers

It is estimated that more than 27 billion disposable diapers (about 3.5 million tons) are used each year in the United States and at least 90% of them end up in landfills. This makes diapers the third largest consumer item found in landfills, after food and beverage containers and paper products.

The average diaper takes about 500 years to degrade in a landfill. And when they do, they release methane and other toxic gasses into the environment. This is on top of the pathogens from the solid waste that could make their way into water sources and pollute our drinking water.

The manufacture of disposable diapers involves the use of numerous chemicals that can be released into the environment. The main culprits are dioxins, furans, dipentene, ethylene benzene, toluene, and xylene, which are classified as carcinogens and endocrine disruptors. They can cause reproductive and developmental problems, and they are also toxic to the liver and kidneys.

Other dangerous chemicals used in disposable diapers include phthalates, polyacrylamides, and TBT (tributyltin). These chemicals can cause skin irritation and contact dermatitis, as well as allergies. They can also be absorbed through the skin, where they can accumulate in the body over time.

Plastic shopping bags

Plastic bags seem like a convenience, but they are actually one of the biggest contributors to plastic pollution. Plastic bags are made from polyethylene, which is a type of plastic that is not biodegradable. This means that when a plastic bag is thrown away, it will never fully break down and will continue to pollute for hundreds of years.

In addition to being non-biodegradable, plastic bags are also very lightweight. This means that they often blow away from landfills and end up in waterways and oceans. Once in the water, the bags can break down into small pieces called microplastics. These tiny pieces of plastic can be eaten by fish and sea animals, which can then be consumed by humans.

The microbes and algae that come into contact with plastic bags in the ocean release food-like aromas that attract turtles and other marine animals, which then mistakenly eat the plastics. The plastics themselves are not digestible and can cause blockages or other health problems in these animals.

Plastic bottles

Single-use plastic bottles and lids are thrown away within minutes of use. This means that they often end up in our oceans and waterways where they can pollute ecosystems and harm the inhabitants.

Seabirds and other marine animals mistake these pieces of plastic for food. They often consume the plastic, not realizing that it will not digest like a fish or crustacean would. This can cause the animal to become sick or even die from the ingestion of plastic.

Even if all plastic bottles were recycled, there would still be a massive amount of plastic waste polluting our environment. The best way to reduce the amount of plastic waste is to break the habit of drinking from plastic bottles.

Plastic food containers and cutlery

The dangers of plastic cutlery are often underestimated. Though they may seem innocuous, plastic knives and forks are sharp and can cause serious injuries to marine animals. Seabirds and turtles are particularly at risk from ingesting plastic cutlery. They can mistake them for food and eat it, leading to blockages in their digestive system.

Equally notorious are plastic food containers, drink stirrers, and plastic straws, which are part of the 36 percent of all plastic packaging that pollute the oceans. If not properly disposed of, reused, or recycled, they can move around the planet, enter huge floating garbage patches, and leach chemicals into food and water supplies.

The best way to avoid these risks is to reduce your reliance on plastic containers altogether. Opt for reusable containers made from glass or stainless steel instead. If you do need to use a disposable container, make sure it's compostable or recyclable.

Plastic Wrappers

Apart from candy wrappers, included in this category is the notorious cling wrap (also known as plastic wrap or saran wrap). Most cling wrap are made from polyvinyl chlorides (PVC), which is a type of plastic that releases dioxins during production, use, and disposal.

Dioxins are highly toxic that it can cause cancer and reproductive and developmental health issues in humans and animals. It is categorized as a Persistent Organic Pollutant (POP) by the U.S. Environmental Protection Agency (EPA), which means it takes a very long time to break down. PVC production is the number one industrial source of human-made dioxin emissions in the United States. That's why PVC is called the poison plastic.

Plastic cups and lids

The cups and lids used in coffee drinks contain thin lining made of plastic, which prevents liquid from leaking out of the container. Although it serves a practical purpose, it also makes the cups and lids difficult to recycle. So, they end up as plastic waste and mistaken for food by fish in the ocean. Eventually, they work their way up the food chain, ending up in our food. This is concerning because the tiny plastic particles can potentially lead to health problems down the line.

Cigarettes

It is estimated that about **6.5 trillion cigarettes are smoked** every year and 4.5 trillion end up as land and marine litter. Unbeknownst to many people, cigarette butts (filters) are made of a type of plastic called cellulose acetate, which is non-biodegradable.

Based on The Ocean Conservancy's trash audit, cigarette butts are the most commonly collected item during beach cleanups. Cigarette butts contain toxic compounds, such as nicotine, arsenic, lead, and polyaromatic hydrocarbons, which can cause cancer, reproductive toxicity, and other health problems.

These toxins can leach out of the cigarette butt and contaminate soil and water. They can also be ingested by animals. So, aside from being unsightly and toxic, cigarette butts also contribute to plastic pollution in a massive way.

Balloons and balloon sticks

Although we don't use balloons on a daily basis, we use them often enough on many occasions and events. Many holiday festivities, sporting events, weddings, and other celebrations culminate with the release of helium-filled balloons into the sky.

Every time a balloon is released into the air, it stays aloft for weeks. They drift for a while and travel hundreds of miles. And we all know that what goes up must come down. When balloons fall to the ground, they often end up in the ocean and waterways.

Two seemingly harmless types of balloons are Mylar and latex balloons. Mylar is more commonly known as foil balloons. They're made of polyethylene terephthalate (PET). Mylar balloons are shiny with reflective surface because of the metallic coating on the nylon sheets. The seams of these balloons are often not well-sealed, which can lead to the release of helium gas and plastic fragments.

Manufacturers of latex balloons claim that the liquid rubber they use are biodegradable, but they're just misleading the consumers. The truth is that they add plasticizers or other chemical additives to the latex to stop or slow down the biodegradation process. Moreover, synthetic latex balloons are made of neoprene, which is a petroleum derivative. It's the same material used to make wetsuits for scuba diving. And just like regular plastics, neoprene will degrade into smaller pieces of plastic over a long period of time—long enough for marine and wildlife mistake them for food.

The seemingly fun and harmless balloons are actually deadly litter. Latex pieces resemble jellyfish or small fish, which make them attractive to bigger marine animals for food. Over time, plastic debris from balloons become coated with algae and microbes that appear as food to sea turtles and other animals.

And because pieces of latex balloons are soft and pliable, they can easily get into the stomach cavity of animals and they can cause intestinal obstruction, which can lead to their deaths.

In addition to the environmental impact of popped balloons, their release is also banned in some states and countries due to the hazard they pose to aviation. However, despite bans and public awareness campaigns, balloons continue to be one of the most commonly found among plastic debris in landfills. Coastal cleanups regularly turn up balloon fragments, and volunteers have even found them floating in the middle of the ocean.

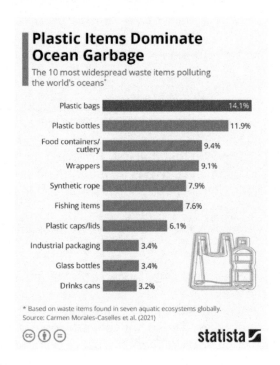

Plastic Items Dominate Ocean Garbage

The 10 most widespread waste items polluting the world's oceans*

Item	Percentage
Plastic bags	14.1%
Plastic bottles	11.9%
Food containers/cutlery	9.4%
Wrappers	9.1%
Synthetic rope	7.9%
Fishing items	7.6%
Plastic caps/lids	6.1%
Industrial packaging	3.4%
Glass bottles	3.4%
Drinks cans	3.2%

* Based on waste items found in seven aquatic ecosystems globally.
Source: Carmen Morales-Caselles et al. (2021)

statista

Source: https://www.statista.com/chart/25056/waste-items-polluting-oceans/

CHAPTER 4: PLASTICS IN RETROGRADE—DEVASTATING IMPACT

ENVIRONMENTAL IMPACT

SEA

The damage caused by plastic pollution is evident throughout the world's oceans. Plastics have been found in the stomachs of marine animals ranging from sea turtles to dolphins to whales. In addition, vast amounts of plastic debris can be seen floating on the surface of the water or washing up on shorelines.

One of the most alarming aspects of plastic pollution is its persistence. Plastic takes centuries to degrade, and even when it does break down, it produces toxic microplastics that contaminate soil and water. These particles are then ingested by fish and other marine animals, leading to their deaths.

Plastic debris can entangle and kill marine animals, interrupt the food chain, and damage coral reefs. The presence of plastics in the ocean creates disruptions in the delicate balance of these ecosystems.

The disruption in the environment where marine species live in has three possibilities and none of them are desirable.

- They can migrate to other places that are much more conducive for survival, albeit temporarily. No matter where they go, plastic pollution will catch up to them.

- They can adapt to the changes in their habitat. However, it's highly unlikely that marine animals would be able to use plastic debris as food. Besides, there's no avoiding plastics—not when millions of tons of plastics are dumped in the ocean every year.

- They can die in many different ways—suffocation, entanglement, starvation and, poisoning.

How did it even come to this? Two words—unbalanced ecosystems.

The marine and coastal areas have a great variety of habitats, ranging from the open ocean to coral reefs, mangroves, and seagrasses. These habitats provide different niches that support a wide range of species, all of which interact with each other in complex ways. It's an environment with rich biodiversity where marine animals and plants have a symbiotic relationship.

The ecosystems that exist in the marine and coastal environment provide significant value to humans and other life forms on Earth. They provide food, nutrients, and mineral resources. They also regulate the climate, help maintain water quality, and support breeding grounds.

Because of the interconnectedness of the aquatic and terrestrial systems, changes in one can have a devastating impact on the other. And one of the most notorious disruptors of this harmonious system is plastic pollution.

Environments are constantly changing, but when natural systems are disrupted to the point of destruction, even evolutionary adaptations of marine species are unlikely. This is because plastic is toxic and has no place in the aquatic ecosystem.

Only 6 percent of all the plastics that reach the oceans float for a while. These are large pieces of plastics that wash up more easily. Along the way, marine animals and coral become entangled in plastic items. Fish mistake them for food. As a result, animals die and coral become diseased.

A staggering 94% disappears beneath the waves and into the ocean floor. The bulk of the plastics sinks and degrades over time into microplastics. This is the start of the disruption, which leads to unbalanced ecosystems down under.

Evidently, human activities can upset this delicate balance, often with disastrous results. Over 75% of plastic litter that end up in the waters come from land-based sources. They are accumulated largely from residential and industrial activities, tourism, and other economic and recreational activities.

Accidental disposal of plastic litter can also happen from maritime transportation activities, but what's really appalling is that there are some marine vessels that intentionally dump plastic waste into the ocean with an accumulation rate of more than 6.5 million tons per year.

LAND

Microplastics are a pervasive pollutant and their ecological implications are just starting to be understood. What's even more worrying is that the disruption does not end in the oceans. It poses a real and present danger to land-based environments. While microplastics are a major concern for ocean life, a study done by German researchers suggests that they also pose a threat to land-based animals, including humans, and may even be more problematic compared to the ocean pollution.

They estimated that microplastic pollution on land is higher by 4 to 23 times than marine microplastic pollution. About one-third of the plastic waste found their way into soils and freshwater, which degrade into microplastics and further disintegrate into nanoplastics, which are less than 0.1 micrometer in size. Plastic waste that are not recycled or used in waste-to-energy facilities end up in landfills. Over time, toxic substances from plastics leach into the soil and water.

Another way microplastics are spread is through sewage systems. Wastewater treatment plants were not designed to remove microplastics from the water and they can easily escape into the environment. Studies suggest that over 90% of the microplastics in wastewater effluent are released into the environment.

Why is this a problem? The gunky leftovers from wastewater treatment known as sewage sludge is used as a fertilizer. It helps to improve the soil structure, add nutrients to the soil, and increase water retention. Sludge also helps to suppress weeds and pests.

Although using sewage sludge as a fertilizer can help reduce the need for chemical fertilizers, it comes with a great cost. A massive amount of microplastics from the sludge end up in the soils and affect the soil fauna and ecosystems in terrible ways.

Take the case of earthworms. These creepy crawly creatures keep the soil healthy. Their castings provide nitrogen and phosphorous to the soil so that crops can grow. When worms create burrows that allow air and water to get through to the plant roots.

If we add microplastics in the equation, it affects the worm's fitness—its ability to survive and reproduce—and the quality of the soil. Worms that were exposed to high levels of microplastics had reduced weight and mobility, and they also had higher levels of toxins in their bodies. The toxins cause the worms to produce fewer eggs, which could lead to population declines in the future and this will have a domino effect on the entire soil ecosystem. This shows that microplastics can have a devastating impact even on land.

AIR

Several research studies from different countries have confirmed what many of us feared—microplastics are present in the air we breathe. Humans breathe in 2,000 to 7,000 microplastic particles every day.

What's even more concerning is that these plastics, which are invisible to the naked eye, travel long distances. This means that even if plastic pollution is concentrated in metropolitan cities, microplastics can end up at least 95 kilometers away. These tiny plastics are so small and light that the wind blow them up the mountains.

In a study conducted in France by researchers from EcoLab, it's estimated that an average of 365 microplastic particles per square meter were found in the Pyrenees Mountains, which is comparable to those found in major cities like Paris. So, it doesn't matter if you live in the city or the countryside, microplastics will always be present.

An interesting discovery from the study was that the plastic bits from the mountains were much smaller in size compared to those from Paris and Dongguan, China, where the microplastics came from clothing and other fabrics. Most of the plastic debris collected from mountain sites were mostly polyethylene and polystyrene (Styrofoam), which are used largely in packing materials and not from fabrics (polypropylene or polyethylene terephthalate)

This all makes sense because polystyrene can be broken down into tiny bits by weather and ultraviolet waves from the sun. The degraded plastic fragments are easily carried by wind, rain, or snow.

Although, the types of plastics have been identified, the source of the microplastic pollution from the mountains are not yet known. It is possible that they come from a variety of sources, aside from packing materials. Microplastics may also be released into the air when plastic products are burned.

Plastic incineration is the process of burning plastic waste to generate electricity enough to power a local grid. Although it's a way to recycle plastic trash, the pollutants released into the air by burning plastic contribute to climate change and stratospheric ozone depletion. They also contaminate bodies of water and soil with toxic chemicals.

Plastic is made up of many harmful chemicals, including carcinogens. When these chemicals are incinerated, they are released into the air in the form of particulate matter, which can cause respiratory problems, heart disease, and other serious health issues.

In addition to being harmful to human health, incineration of plastic also causes environmental damage. Once airborne, these tiny particles can be transported long distances before landing back on the ground or entering the water cycle. Ultimately, incineration is not a safe or environmentally friendly way to dispose of plastic.

What does this all mean? It means the environment and everything in it are exposed to more plastics than earlier realized. Airborne plastics will eventually find their way into land and waterways, which then triggers a disruption in the ecosystems.

The findings also raise concerns about the potential health risks posed by microplastics inhalation by humans and animals.

SOCIAL IMPACT

The ecological impact of plastic pollution is devastating enough. It's evident in how ecosystems are disrupted and marine habitats destroyed. But the destruction doesn't stop at the environmental and ecological levels. It's far worse than that.

The socio-economic impacts of plastic pollution are particularly troubling, as they affect the poorest and most vulnerable members of society. When a significant number of marine animals falls victim to plastic pollution, it can have a devastating effect on local communities that rely on fishing for their livelihoods.

LIVELIHOOD
It's not just an isolated case in a handful of communities. It's an emerging threat around the world. In fact, a recent study found that microplastics are present in nearly all fish caught in the Mediterranean Sea. This means that plastic pollution is also affecting the people who depend on the fishing industry.

The impact of plastic pollution on fishing communities has economic effects. First, it affects the quantity and quality of fish available for catch. Studies have shown that microplastics can reduce fish populations and disrupt their feeding habits. Some fish migrate to safer waters while others die. Those who survive may be contaminated with toxins.

The change in distribution and populations of marine life not only reduces the number of fish available for fishermen to sell, but also makes it more difficult to catch healthy fish fit for consumption. When there are concerns in the quality of fish and seafood, there is a corresponding decrease in demand, which, in turn, can cause a significant drop in revenue.

Billions of people depend on healthy oceans to provide them with a source of food and income. In fact, the world's oceans contribute $1.5 trillion annually to the global economy. It's estimated that this figure could double by 2030.

The Food and Agriculture Organization (FAO) of the United Nations estimates that there are more than 60 million people employed in the fisheries and aquaculture sector worldwide. Most of them are from developing and poor countries where fishing is crucial for food production and economic growth.

When the world's oceans are contaminated by plastics, fisherfolk around the world risk losing their main source of income. This considerably affects their way of life. Even their mental health is affected because they worry about how they will support their families.

TOURISM

Plastic pollution is also a big threat to the tourism industry. Tourism is a huge industry that brings in billions of dollars to countries all over the world. People flock to pristine beaches and fishing sites. It is no secret that healthy, clean surroundings are one of the main draws for tourists. Unfortunately, plastic pollution in beaches and marine habitats reduces the aesthetic value and mars the natural beauty of coastal shores.

Plastic bottles, bags, cups, straws, and food wrappers are some of the most common types of litter found on beaches. They make beaches and other tourist destinations look unsightly and unappealing and can even be dangerous to tourists.

People may be less likely to visit areas that are polluted with plastic, or they may be willing to pay less for tourist activities in such areas.

In some cases, plastic pollution has led to the closure of popular tourist destinations, which is a key part of the local economy. When beaches are closed, it can lead to a loss in tourism revenue. Furthermore, plastic pollution can cause health problems for tourists.

It is important to address the issue of plastic pollution so that it does not continue to have a negative impact on tourism. This will require a concerted effort by governments, businesses, and individuals around the world.

PERSONAL AND HEALTH IMPACT

Every stage of the plastic lifecycle presents risks to human health:

- The extraction and transport of oil and gas and hydraulic fracturing emit a significant volume of toxic substances into the air and water.

- More than 170 fracking chemicals are used to produce feedstocks for plastic. Their impact on human health creates a long list of diseases and maladies, including cancer, auto-immune diseases, reproductive toxicity, gastrointestinal problems, respiratory ailments, and liver failure.

- Refining and transforming fossil fuels into plastic resins releases substances that are highly toxic and carcinogenic.

- The use of plastic products leads to the inhalation or ingestion of microplastics, toxic substances, and chemical additives.

- Plastic waste management processes such as incineration, gasification, and pyrolysis put communities at risk of exposure to toxic emissions.

What's often overlooked is the fact that microplastics can also enter the food chain. This means that we are consuming plastic without even knowing it. **Recent research** suggests that humans consume approximately 5 grams of microplastics every week—that's about the same weight as a credit card.

Several studies looked at the presence of microplastics in food products from around the world and found that plastic was present in a wide variety of foods, including fish, shellfish, meats, grains, fruits, and vegetables. Furthermore, microplastics were present in the water we drink.

As concerns about the potential health risks posed by microplastics are increasing, the World Health Organization (WHO) released a report stating that more research is needed to determine if these particles are harmful and, if so, what kind of risks they may pose. Some previous studies have suggested that microplastics can cause inflammation and damage to the gut and potentially trigger a systemic, but the WHO report says that there is not yet enough evidence to confirm this.

While it's not enough to allay our fears, the WHO acknowledges the need to stop the rise in plastic pollution.

PLASTICS INSIDE US

A study commissioned by **Orb Media** revealed that 83 percent of samples from tap water in 12 countries on 5 continents were contaminated with plastic fibres. For each 500ml sample of tap water, the number of fibers found is anywhere from 1.9 to 4.8 pieces.

Among the countries included in the study, the US had the highest contamination rate at 94.4 percent. It's closely followed by Lebanon at 92.8 percent and India at 82.4 percent.

European countries, which included the UK, Germany, and France, registered the lowest contamination rate at 72%. The findings suggest that billions of people could be drinking water contaminated with microplastics.

Microplastics have also been found to act like magnets, picking up more toxins and pollutants as they are transported by wind and water. They are known to absorb polychlorinated biphenyls, which are now banned in the US. Contaminated microplastics can potentially release toxic substances into the bloodstream and internal organs. This is on top of whatever chemicals are present in the plastics.

There is currently no effective way to remove all the microplastics from water, so until a solution is found, we're bound to continue consuming microplastics through food, water, and air.

MICROPLASTICS IN OUR POOP

There is mounting evidence that microplastics exist in our poop. In a joint study by the Environment Agency Austria and Medical University of Vienna, eight stool samples from eight countries tested positive for the presence of different types of plastics in human excrements—about 20 plastic particles per 10 grams of stool.

All of the stool sample contained polypropylene and polyethylene-terephthalate particles (PET), which are the types of plastics used in the manufacture of plastic bottles and caps. This suggests that the participants were exposed to microplastics by eating food wrapped in plastic or drinking from plastic bottles.

In another study on the occurrence of microplastics on infant and adult feces, it was discovered that microplastics found in baby feces were 10 times higher than in adult feces.

The majority of studies on microplastics and human health have been focused on exposure to them through drinking water. But now there's growing evidence that we're also exposed to them through other routes, including ingestion of food and contact with our skin.

How many of these plastic particles are entering our bloodstream and lymphatic system? Will they penetrate the liver? Research studies on humans are scarce on this topic, however, in studies done on animals, there is evidence that microplastics can cause liver stress and intestinal damage.

Scientific studies have shown that anything smaller than 150 microns can penetrate the gut wall and enter the blood cells and organs. Microplastics come in different sizes, but the smallest found is 0.7 microns. This tells us that it's highly possible that microplastics can invade our bodies, even our internal organs.

And true enough, Professor Dick Vethaak, an ecotoxicologist at Vrije Universiteit Amsterdam in the Netherlands has discovered that microplastics have been found in the human blood, largely from drinking water and beverages from plastic bottles.

Unfortunately, most water filters do not remove microplastics. And while there are a few labs in the world that can test for them, there is no regulatory body that requires manufacturers to disclose whether their products contain microplastics.

More research is needed to determine how long microplastics remain in the blood and organs and what health effects they may have in the long term.

REPRODUCTIVE TOXICITY

Microplastics have been shown to have a variety of potential negative effects on human health, from causing gastrointestinal issues to interfering with hormone production. But perhaps the most devasting is the potential to cause cancer and infertility.

One potential health concern associated with microplastics is their impact on reproductive health and fertility. Microplastics and nanoplastics may interfere with normal hormone function, which could lead to problems with reproduction. Additionally, the chemicals in plastic can potentially damage cells and tissues. This could cause infertility or other reproductive health issues.

In a study published on the American Journal of Men's Health, the results suggest that microplastics may be a significant cause of infertility in men by damaging sperm and affecting semen quality.

PHTHALATE SYNDROME

Reproductive and environmental epidemiologist Dr. Shanna Swan and colleagues published a groundbreaking research that revealed an astonishing discovery—sperm levels among men in Western countries have declined by more than 50 percent in the last 40 years. All findings and methodology of research study are discussed in the book, *Count Down*.

Upon examining 185 studies involving 45,000 healthy male participants, they came to the conclusion that chemical exposures and lifestyle are affecting not just sexual development, but also fertility.

Environmental chemicals, such as those that leach from plastic products, interfere with the body's natural hormones by disrupting the production and distribution of testosterone, estrogen, or thyroid hormones.

Since endocrine-disrupting chemicals are everywhere, they are virtually unavoidable. A growing number of American couples may be unknowingly suffering from *phthalate syndrome*, a condition caused by exposure to phthalates, which are a group of toxic chemicals commonly found in processed food, personal care products, and other consumer goods.

Dr. Swan's research suggests that there is a strong link between prenatal phthalate exposure and human reproductive development. Exposure to these chemicals is especially risky to pregnant women.

A study published in Environmental International suggests that these tiny pieces of plastic were detected in human placenta. This means that microplastics are able to cross the placenta and enter the fetus.

The researchers found that microplastics were present in the placental tissue and in the fetuses themselves. This has health implications in early pregnancy when the male fetus' genitals are developing very rapidly.

Even a small amount of phthalates has the ability to interfere with the hormones that are needed for development. For example, the male fetus needs a certain amount of testosterone at the right time for normal development of the sex organ.

According to Dr. Swan, if the mother is exposed to phthalates, it can decrease testosterone production and the male child will not develop normally. This can result in the baby having a smaller penis and be less completely masculinized, which can potentially increase gender fluidity. The same endocrine-disrupting chemicals might also affect brain development.

Phthalate syndrome is still relatively new, and more research is needed to determine its full extent and effects. However, Dr. Swan's work provides some of the first evidence that this condition may be a serious public health concern that needs to be addressed as the global production of plastics is accelerating at an unprecedented pace.

CANCER

Animals exposed to microplastics had disrupted metabolic function—they have higher levels of blood glucose and cholesterol, as well as a higher body mass index. They also showed increased signs of inflammation and oxidative stress. While the findings need to be confirmed in humans, they suggest that exposure to microplastics could have serious consequences for human health.

Oxidative stress is a process that can damage cells. It occurs when there is an imbalance between the production of free radicals and the ability of the body to counteract or repair the damage. It has been linked to a range of health problems, including cancer, heart disease, and Alzheimer's disease.

Free radicals are unstable molecules that can cause oxidative damage to cells. The body produces free radicals as a normal part of metabolism, but environmental factors, such as pollution and smoking, can also increase their number. They can also interfere with the normal functioning of cells and increase the risk of health problems.

Microplastics can cause inflammation by entering the body and interacting with cells. When microplastics enter the body, they can release toxins that cause inflammation. Microplastics can also attract bacteria, which can lead to inflammation.

Inflammation is a natural response to injury or infection. When it persists, it can lead to chronic diseases such as cancer, diabetes, and heart disease. Microplastics may contribute to chronic inflammation by causing cell damage and releasing toxins.

GETTING MICROPLASTICS OUT OF OUR SYSTEM

The presence of tiny plastic particles in our bloodstream is proof of how pervasive and intrusive these microplastics are. They're pretty much everywhere, and the way to protect ourselves is to reduce our exposure to them.

Our exposure levels to plastics are at an all-time high because of the prevalent use of plastic food packaging as well as eating foods that are contaminated with plastic chemicals. Not even the Food and Drug Authority (FDA) can protect us because under their flawed regulatory system, companies are allowed to use chemicals in food packaging without being required to release toxicological data on the chemicals that can transfer to food.

What's more, the risk assessment method used by federal agencies is not only outdated, but also singularly focuses on the dangers of high doses of chemicals. It doesn't take into account the health risks associated with the consumption of low doses of plastic chemicals over time. The lack of transparency puts everyone at risk of contamination.

When microplastics enter the body, it is difficult to get them out of the system. Once they circulate in the bloodstream, they are transported to different parts of the body. Some of them get stuck in the lungs, while others accumulate in the kidneys and liver. Some of the microplastics are filtered and expelled, but what happens with those that stay in the system?

The only way to effectively **remove microplastics from the bloodstream** is through medical procedures such as an IVC (inferior vena cava) filter or dialysis. Clearly, this is not the solution that we want. The best way to protect yourself from the harmful effects of plastic pollution is to avoid plastic as much as possible. As they say, prevention is better than cure.

Here are practical ways to reduce exposure to plastic:

1. Drink tap water instead of bottled water.

2. Heat food using the stove or oven instead of microwaving plastic containers.

3. Use glass containers, silicone, or foil to store food instead of plastic food containers.

4. Eat fresh food or whole foods that are either organic or sourced from local farmers markets instead of overly processed food that are wrapped in plastic packaging.

5. Be aware of where your food is coming from. Some places have higher levels of plastic pollution than others, so it's best to avoid seafood and other foods that are likely to be contaminated with plastic particles.

Avoid seafoods with the highest level of microplastics, which include clams, oysters, scallops, and mussels.

6. Vacuum your house regularly to get rid of dust that may contain plastic and chemicals like phthalates. Don't let the surfaces get dusty, as they can be inhaled. It's recommended to use a vacuum cleaner with a HEPA filter. You can also use an air purifier with an air filter and an ionizer.

7. Work with your community to help reduce the use of single-use plastics. Partner with your local recycling centers and environmental non-profit organizations and advocates. As a group, your voice is much louder and more impactful—enough to make your local representatives listen.

8. Encourage chain stores to implement a plastic bottle deposit program and offer refill options.

9. Support legislation that limits the use of single-use plastic products, no matter the city, state, or country.

MICROPLASTIC FILTRATION

Water treatment plants are effective in removing microplastics from water sources. However, the level of efficiency varies considerably across water treatment and filtration technologies. Primary treatment of wastewater is reported to effectively remove 16.5 to 98.4 percent microplastics, while secondary treatment has a microplastics removal efficiency of 78.1 to 100 percent. Tertiary treatment has an efficiency ranging from 87.3 percent to 99.9 percent microplastics.

This means that water treatment processes like filtration, coagulation, sedimentation, and flocculation work well to keep public drinking water safe and clean.

But there's just one problem—not all places have high microplastic removal efficiency, as seen from the reported percentages. This means that the level of microplastics in water depends on where you live.

If you live in a city with a low incidence of microplastic contaminants and water treatment is effective in filtering out microplastics from water sources, then you have one less plastic-related problem to solve.

If you live in an area with high levels of microplastics in the water and your city has a poor water treatment facility, then you cannot just rest your fate in the hands of your municipal water treatment plant. Until it improves its microplastics removal efficiency to at least 99 percent, you can use a home filtration system that will serve as an added layer of defense to reduce your exposure to and consumption of microplastics.

Not all home water filter devices can filter microplastics, much less nanoplastics. While carbon block filters and granular activated carbon filters can effectively remove particles as small as 5 millimeters, they cannot filter smaller plastic particles.

This brings us to the most viable option—**reverse osmosis system**.

Reverse osmosis is an effective filtration method to remove microplastics and nanoplastics from water. This process works by using a high-pressure pump to force water through a semi-permeable membrane. The pores of the membrane are small enough to allow water molecules to pass through but too small for microplastics to pass. This process can remove up to 99% of microplastics from water.

In a large-scale water treatment operation, reverse osmosis is a lot more expensive than standard filtration as it requires a great deal of energy to push water through a filter. This is why not all water treatment plants use reverse osmosis.

However, in a small-scale setup, like in a home or a small office, a reverse osmosis filtration system is reasonably priced for what it can do. It can significantly reduce the microplastics that you unknowingly consume.

While reverse osmosis systems are more expensive than traditional filtration systems, they are still relatively affordable, especially when compared to the cost of bottled water consume over time. Plus, they offer a much higher level of protection against microplastics and other contaminants. The filtered water can then be used for drinking, cooking, and bathing. It's a good start if you want to protect yourself and your family from microplastic ingestion due to bottled water.

CHAPTER 5: THE GAMEPLAN— AWARENESS & ACTION

The sheer scale of the plastic pollution problem can be daunting—and it can be difficult to know where to start fixing it. On the upside, there's growing awareness of the seriousness of the problem and people are recognizing the need for a change.

But is it too late to fix it? Have we already produced more than enough plastic to cause irreversible damage? With global plastic production projected to reach 483.19 million metric tons by 2030, are we now royally screwed?

With plastic production outpacing our ability to collect plastic trash and properly dispose of them, it's becoming increasingly difficult to see the light at the end of a very filthy tunnel. Even if we manage to collect all the plastic waste, where in the world should we put them?

The question bears repeating: Is it too late to fix the plastic pollution problem?

Ocean Conservancy's chief scientist George Leonard, **said it best** when he stated that if we don't get the problem under control, the entire marine food web would be contaminated with plastic waste. If we fail to catch up, then it will be too late and we can expect a future where plastic litter will be embedded in the ocean forever.

It will take more than a heavy dose of optimism to move the needle. We need systemic change if we want to address this crisis. Fixing the problem requires a change in the way we produce, use, and discard plastic.

That means moving away from disposable plastics and investing in sustainable alternatives. It won't be easy, but it's not too late.

SOLUTIONS BASED ON CIRCULAR ECONOMY

Plastic is one of the most ubiquitous materials on Earth. Most products that we use on a daily basis are made from plastic or have plastic components in them. But our love affair with this miracle material has come at a cost: it's destroying our planet.

The good news is that we have the power to fix this problem. The solution to the plastic crisis is circularity—turning plastic waste into valuable products and materials.

Circular economy is a system where waste and resource depletion are minimized. It is an alternative to the traditional linear economy, where resources are used once and then discarded.

PLASTIC WASTE MANAGEMENT IN CIRCULAR ECONOMY

The circular economy model aims to achieve the following:

1. Eliminate waste and eradicate pollution.

Waste and pollution are two of the biggest problems facing the world today. They not only have a negative impact on the environment, but also cost businesses and governments billions of dollars each year. Fortunately, there are ways to reduce or eliminate waste and pollution that are both environmentally and economically sustainable.

The success of a circular economy hinges on design from the start of the product life cycle. One example is the use of "cradle-to-cradle" design, which creates products that can be easily recycled or reused. Another example is the sharing economy, which encourages people to share goods and services instead of buying new ones.

The benefits of a circular economy can help to reduce greenhouse gas emissions, conserve resources, create jobs, and improve public health. It also has the potential to make businesses more sustainable and profitable.

2. Circulate resources and products at their highest value so nothing becomes waste.

A circular economy means maximizing the reuse, recycling, and restoration of products and conservation of valuable resources—from buying recycled products to investing in renewable energy. Governments can help by creating policies that incentivize sustainable practices. Businesses can get involved by designing products for reuse and recycling. And everyday citizens can make a difference by making simple changes in their daily habits.

3. Allow nature to regenerate.

In order for our planet to regenerate, we must support natural processes, maintain natural ecosystems, and leave more room for nature to thrive. It is crucial that we take care of our planet and work together to restore the Earth's natural balance.

We can do our part by reducing our consumption, composting, recycling, and using less plastic. We also need to plant more trees and create wildlife habitats. If we all pitch in and do our part, we can make a real difference in restoring the Earth's health.

RETHINKING REDUCE, REUSE, RECYCLE

Though it is not possible to eliminate plastic waste altogether, reducing the amount of plastic produced could go a long way in mitigating the pollution it causes. This requires a global campaign where everyone—from government officials to organizations to communities to private citizens—needs to do their part in reducing the amount of plastic waste.

There has to be a concerted program that will invigorate the plastic waste movement. The existing Reduce, Reuse, Recycle (3Rs) program we have is a waste management strategy that encourages people to reduce the amount of waste they produce, reuse items whenever possible, and recycle materials that would otherwise be thrown away. The program has been around for a long time and is seen as the gold standard for helping to protect our environment. But is it enough?

Although the 3Rs program is effective and successful in some ways, this campaign has not kept up with the enormity of the global plastic pollution problem. In order to face the pollution crisis, a more dynamic global 3Rs program is needed that will lessen the impact of human activities.

There is still much to be done to bring the program up to speed with the rapid destruction that's happening. For one, the 3Rs program needs to be more vigorously promoted so that everyone is aware of it and can participate in it on a much larger scale. People need to be taught how to reduce their waste production and recycle properly.

In addition, more money needs to be invested in recycling facilities so that there is an infrastructure in place to handle all the recyclable materials that are being produced. Technology will play a significant role in reducing plastic consumption and promoting waste reduction strategies.

The Reduce, Reuse, and Recycle program will still be the cornerstone of sustainability in the fight against plastic pollution. It just needs to be massively tweaked to keep up with the rising threat of plastic pollution.

DECREASE PLASTIC FOOTPRINT: REFUSE, REDUCE AND REUSE

In its simplest sense, "Reduce" refers to cutting back on the plastic waste we generate. This means using less throwaway plastic. When we reduce our use of plastic, we stop the problem at its source.

Plastic is often used for single-use items, such as grocery bags, straws, cups, and utensils. The majority of this plastic waste isn't recycled and ends up in our landfills, oceans, and waterways. By using less of these items, we can reduce plastic litter in the first place.

If every person made just a few small changes to their everyday plastic habits, we could make a real difference in reducing the amount of plastic waste produced each year.

What sort of changes can individuals do at this level?

Giving up plastic may seem like a daunting task, but there are plenty of ways to reduce your plastic consumption without making drastic changes to your lifestyle. Start by evaluating the amount of plastic you use on a daily basis and finding substitutes for common items made from plastic.

Reducing your plastic footprint is not something that you do all at once. You need to take small steps until you develop a habit. Gradually, you'll be able to reduce the amount of plastic you consume until it becomes a zero-plastic lifestyle, or at least very close to it.

If you try to make too many changes at once, you may become overwhelmed and discouraged. Start by making a list of items in different categories:

- **Bathroom Products**
- **Kitchen**
- **Clothing, Bedding & Laundry**
- **Children**
- **Workplace**
- **Pets**
- **Community**

Add more to your list (or category) and work towards eliminating as much plastic from your life as possible.

BATHROOM PRODUCTS

A good place to start your plastic-free journey is in the bathroom. The packaging for many common bathroom products is made of plastic. This includes items like shampoo, conditioner, soap, lotion, and toothpaste, among others.

Not all the plastic bottles and containers are recyclable and most recycling centers will not accept them because they cannot be recycled into new products. This means that the majority of these plastics end up in landfills and oceans.

While you are not expected to give up using shampoo, conditioner, and toiletries, you can reduce your plastic footprint by switching to more sustainable options.

SWITCH TO REFILLABLES

When it comes to reducing plastic waste, refillable shampoo and conditioner bottles are a great option. Not only do they help cut down on the amount of plastic that ends up in landfills and oceans, but they can also save you money in the long run.

There's a growing number of small, independent brands that allow their customers to refill shampoo and conditioner containers. This can be a great way to reduce plastic consumption, as many people go through a lot of shampoo and conditioner each month. As a result, this small change helps you cut down on plastic waste.

Even big-name companies like Unilever, Tata Harper, Amika, and other brands now offer refillable options for some of their products, including deodorants. This makes it easy to keep your bottle topped off.

Most refillable items come with a reusable container which you can reuse over and over again. This eliminates the need to buy new containers every time you need to purchase a new product. What's even more eco-friendly is if you use glass bottles or jars with pumps.

In some places, shops have refill stations where you bring your own bottle or container to fill with shampoo or conditioner. This eliminates the need for wasteful packaging.

In a nutshell, if you're looking for an eco-friendly and affordable way to reduce your reliance on plastic packaging for bathroom products, consider using refillable shampoo and conditioner bottles.

USE SOAP AND SHAMPOO BAR (AND NAKED DEODORANT)

Any self-respecting individual who has become aware of the dangers of plastic and the negative impact it has on the environment, will try to get rid of as much plastic as possible from their lives, including in their bathroom. One way people are doing this is by switching to solid soaps and shampoos with no plastic packaging—or no packaging at all.

There are a number of benefits to using solid soaps and shampoos. For one, they are much more sustainable than traditional liquid soaps and shampoos. They also tend to be more affordable in the long run, since you don't have to buy new bottles every time you run out of soap or shampoo. Solid soaps and shampoos also last a lot longer than traditional liquid soaps and shampoos, meaning you don't have to use as much product each time you bathe or wash your hair.

Even deodorants now come in bars with compostable paper packaging. They are called zero-waste deodorant, which is a type of deodorant that doesn't come in a disposable plastic container. This means that there is no packaging to throw away, and the deodorant can be used until it's gone.

USE NATURAL SPONGES FOR BATHING

Bath sponges come in all shapes and sizes and they can be made from natural or synthetic materials—mesh sponges, natural sea sponges, loofah sponges, and synthetic sponges.

Mesh sponges are typically made from nylon or polyester mesh. Natural sea sponges are harvested from the ocean while loofah sponges are made from the dried fruit of the Loofah plant.

Based on what's available in the market, it's an easy decision to switch to sea sponge or loofah because these products are much more eco-friendly than nylon sponges. They are made from natural materials, so they don't require any harsh chemicals to be produced. They biodegrade quickly, making them a more sustainable option in the long run.

AVOID MICROBREADS

Microbeads are tiny pieces of plastic that are less than 5 millimeters in size. They are used as exfoliants in personal care products, such as face wash, toothpaste, soap, and shampoo.

Despite their small size, microbeads are a major source of marine pollution. They can easily enter waterways through wastewater treatment plants and then be ingested by fish and other animals under the sea. Studies have shown that microbeads can accumulate toxins like PCBs and pesticides, which can then be transferred to the animals that eat them.

In response to the growing concern over microbead pollution, **The Microbead-Free Waters Act of 2015** was signed into law and took effect in 2017. This law prohibits the manufacturing, packaging, and distribution of rinse-off cosmetics that contain microbeads.

Always read the ingredient list on personal care products before buying them so you can avoid using microbeads. If you see the following plastics on the list, then the product is likely to have microbeads in them.

- Polyethylene (PE)
- Polypropylene (PP)
- Polyethylene terephthalate (PET)
- Polymethyl methacrylate (PMMA)
- Polytetrafluoroethylene (PTFE)
- Nylon

MAKE YOUR OWN TOOTHPASTE

Are you looking for a toothpaste without microbeads? Making your own toothpaste is a great way to avoid these plastic beads. All you need are a few simple ingredients that you can find in your kitchen.

To make toothpaste, start by mixing together baking soda and water. Add in some peppermint extract or essential oil for flavor. You can also add in a pinch of sea salt if you need more abrasiveness. Stir until the mixture forms a thick paste.

You can store your homemade toothpaste in a small jar or container. It will last for several weeks, so you can make a batch and use it as needed.

Some homemade toothpaste recipes require xylitol and bentonite clay. Xylitol is a natural antibacterial and anti-inflammatory agent. It also neutralizes the pH of the mouth, making it less hospitable to bacteria. Bentonite clay, on the other hand, helps to remineralize teeth, which can help to prevent cavities.

SHAVE LIKE IT'S THE 1900s
Disposable single-use razors can't be recycled and thus create a lot of waste. Buy yourself a safety razor instead! Although safety razors nowadays come with plastic handles, there are still

non-plastic options like metal, steel, or wooden handle, which can be reused for years, just like what people do in the early 1900s.

Safety razors are reusable, so you only need to buy replacement blades occasionally. Disposable razors may seem like a more convenient option, but they're actually much worse for the environment.

For the ladies, it's a little more challenging to find hair removal products without plastic in them. Typical waxing requires the use of plastic strips and wax that come in plastic packaging. A Do-It-Yourself approach using sugar-based wax to remove hair is a great alternative that will definitely reduce your plastic footprint.

USE PLASTIC-FREE MAKE-UP BRANDS

The cosmetics industry has been under fire in recent years for the amount of plastic waste it produces. One of the main sources of this waste is the plastic packaging that products come in. Packaging accounts for a large percentage of the total weight of a product.

For example, the actual lipstick typically weighs around 3-5 grams, but its packaging can weigh 10-30 grams, depending on the brand. This means that more than half the weight of a lipstick is packaging.

The sad part is that much of this packaging is made from plastic, which is not biodegradable. It will eventually end up in landfill or in our oceans. While there are calls for cosmetics companies to use more recyclable materials for their packaging, such as cardboard, metal tin cans, and glass, there's little innovation in this area.

Some make-up products with plastic-free alternatives include reusable cotton pads, compostable sponges, and lip balm in biodegradable cardboard tubes.

USE BAMBOO COTTON BUDS

Plastic-stemmed cotton buds are banned in Scotland, as the country clamps down on single-use plastics. The ban prohibits shops from selling the items, with offenders facing a fine. The move comes after it was revealed that around 1.8 billion plastic-stemmed cotton buds are used in the UK every year, with most of them ending up in landfill or being flushed down the toilet and causing blockages. The new law will see Scotland join a number of other countries - including Ireland and France - in banning the sale of cotton buds.

In the United States, there's no law banning the selling of plastic-stemmed cotton buds. However, consumers now have a sustainable option in bamboo cotton buds, such as BOONBOO cotton swabs. The bamboo stem is a natural material that is biodegradable and compostable. The cotton is also organic and fair trade. These cotton buds are a better choice for the environment than traditional cotton buds with plastic stems.

GIVE REUSABLE MENSTRUAL CUP A CHANCE

It may come as a surprise to many people that tampons and sanitary pads contain plastic. They are made of a blend of rayon and cotton. Conventionally grown cotton is one of the most chemically dependent crops in the world and uses large amounts of pesticides, herbicides, and fertilizers. These chemicals are known to contaminate water supplies and damage ecosystems.

The majority of tampons and pads also contain non-biodegradable plastic fibers which can take centuries to break down in landfills. The average woman will use at least 12,000 tampons or pads in her lifetime. When disposed of, tampons and pads add to the growing problem of microplastics pollution.

What's the alternative? A reusable menstrual cup that is made out of silicone. Unlike disposable pads and tampons, the menstrual cup like Mooncup can be used for up to 10 years and it only needs to be washed with soap and water. So, it is cheaper in the long run because women don't have to keep buying disposable pads or tampons.

However, some women find menstrual cups uncomfortable or difficult to use. There are also some logistical concerns with using a menstrual cup—they can be difficult to keep clean, and they need to be emptied several times a day.

Some women simply just want to stick with their trusty tampons. Good thing there are now biodegradable, compostable, reusable (applicator) and even recyclable tampon options. Even switching to these more sustainable options can help move the needle in the fight against plastic pollution.

CLOTHING, BEDDING, AND LAUNDRY

The clothes in your closet and the sheets on your bed, believe it or not, also contain plastic—polyester, to be exact. It's a type of fabric that is made from petrochemicals, specifically, polyethylene terephthalate (PET). It's the perfect material for fast fashion. It's abundant and cheap.

These small strands of plastic fabric, which are invisible to the naked eye, are released into the air and into the lakes and oceans when clothes are washed. They accumulate in the environment and can enter the food chain.

Although it appears like this is a losing battle—after all, we need to wear clothes and use bed sheets—there are still ways to minimize our plastic footprint in this regard.

BUY CLOTHES MADE FROM SUSTAINABLE MATERIALS

The fashion industry is one of the world's most polluting industries, and the fast fashion trend isn't helping. But some companies are starting to heed the call for a more sustainable clothing line.

H&M, for instance, partnered with the Ellen MacArthur Foundation, Greenpeace, and other organizations to launch the "Conscious Exclusive" line, which includes clothes made from sustainable materials.

Stella McCartney's Adidas Primeknit collection features shoes made from recycled ocean plastic. The shoes are made of yarn that is created by melting down old plastic bottles found in the ocean. This reduces the reliance on virgin materials and also helps to clean up the environment. It contains at least 25% recycled content.

Other clothing brands that use sustainable materials in their products include Patagonia, Pact, Beyond Retro, Wolven, and Rapanui, among others.

There are several sustainable materials available, so you can feel good about your clothing choices and help reduce your plastic footprint too. Always read the label of the clothes you are buying and look for any of the following:

Organic Cotton

Organic cotton is a natural fiber that is grown without the use of synthetic fertilizers, pesticides, or other chemicals. It is produced by farmers who adhere to strict organic standards set by the United States Department of Agriculture (USDA). Organic cotton is soft, durable, and breathable, making it a popular choice for clothing, bedding, and other home textiles.

Tencel

Tencel is a natural fiber made from the cellulose of wood pulp. It is a sustainable resource that is biodegradable and recyclable. Tencel is very soft and has a luxurious drape. It is also very absorbent and moisture-wicking. Tencel is perfect for underwear, sheets, and baby clothes.

Bamboo

Bamboo fabric is an increasingly popular choice for eco-conscious clothing. The fabric is made from the pulp of bamboo plants, which makes it a sustainable resource. Bamboo fabric is soft, breathable, and comfortable to wear. It is also anti-microbial and resistant to odor.

Hemp

Hemp fiber has been used for clothing for thousands of years. Hemp is a durable, breathable fabric that is also environmentally friendly. Hemp can be grown without the use of pesticides or herbicides, and it requires less water than other crops. Hemp fabric is also biodegradable and recyclable.

UPCYCLE CLOTHES FROM DISCARDED GARMENTS

There are many ways to upcycle clothes from discarded garments. One way is to cut the fabric into small pieces and use it as stuffing for a pillow or duvet. Another way is to cut the fabric into strips and use it as a border for a quilt. You can also cut the fabric into squares and make a patchwork quilt. Another option is to make a rag rug out of the fabric. You can also make clothing out of the fabric, such as a skirt, shirt, or dress.

If you do not have the resources or skills to upcycle clothes, you can support clothing brands that upcycle old garments to create new clothes. Brands that sell reused, repurposed, recycled, vintage, and upcycled clothing include Repainted, Amour Vert, Beyond Retro, Urban Outfitters, Wolf & Badger, Farm Rio, and Re/Done, among others.

USE WASHING MESH BAGS AND LAUNDRY BALLS

A typical load of laundry emits more than 1,600 fibers into the environment. While many of these fibers are captured by wastewater treatment plants, some still escape and end up in waterways and eventually the ocean.

To help reduce the amount of microfibers released into the air, consider using a washing mesh bag. Mesh bags can capture 54% to 78% of the fibers from synthetic clothes during the wash cycle.

When shopping for a washing mesh bag, be sure to look for one made from 100% recycled materials. There are a number of great options available online, and most cost between $30 and $50. Two of the more popular brands of mesh bags are Guppyfriend and XFiltra filter.

Another product that helps reduce microfibers that end up in the oceans is the Cora Ball, a laundry ball made from recycled materials that is designed to help keep clothes lint-free. The ball catches and traps microfibers into a fuzz as they come off of clothes in the wash cycle. The Cora Ball can be used with both front- and top-loading washing machines and is said to be effective at removing up to 90% of microfibers from the wash.

In a study involving 97 homes with washing machines that come with built-in filters, it was found to be effective in capturing microfibers with lint capture of 6.4 grams weekly. This is equivalent to 179,2000 to 2,707,200 microfibers. Although it's a small-scale study, it has the potential to help significantly reduce microfiber emissions from washing clothes when applied at a bigger scale.

TRY BEDDINGS MADE FROM RECYCLED MATERIALS

Just like clothes, bedsheets, covers, blankets, pillows, cushions, and duvets all contain microplastics. The types of plastics most commonly found in beddings are polyester, acrylic and polypropylene. When these items are washed or exposed to heat or sunlight, they can release tiny pieces of plastic into the air and that's how they contribute to plastic pollution.

For a plastic-free sleep, consider using beddings, pillows, and duvets made from natural materials and goose down. Another option you can try is a new type of bedding made from recycled microfibre which is made from waste plastic PET bottles. The process to create this type of bedding requires less energy, and results in less plastic waste. This innovation hopes to inspire others to find new ways to recycle plastic and reduce the amount of waste that ends up in landfills and oceans.

Companies like Scoom and Weaver Green are turning the problem into a solution as their products are made from recycled materials, including post-consumer plastics. This means that the products are made from materials that would otherwise end up in a landfill. As this gets more traction from consumers, we can hope for the products to become available mainstream.

KITCHEN PRODUCTS

Plastic is a common material used in many kitchen products. Naturally, there are concerns about their potential negative effects of using plastic products in the kitchen. Some of the main concerns include the release of chemicals and toxins into food and drinks, and the impact on wildlife.

Evidently, there are alternatives to using plastic products in the kitchen. Glass, stainless steel, and silicone are all safe materials that can be used for food storage, cooking, and baking. Reusable grocery bags made from natural materials such as cotton, bamboo, and hemp are alternative options

Making a few simple changes can help reduce your dependence on plastic kitchen products. By choosing safer, non-toxic materials, and opting for reusable items whenever possible, you can help keep your family healthy and protect the environment at the same time.

DITCH THE PLASTIC BAGS WHEN GROCERY SHOPPING

The average person in the United States uses about 365 plastic bags a year. This not only leads to a massive plastic waste, but it also requires a lot of oil to produce—about 12 million barrels. As we know, oil is a non-renewable resource and global oil reserves are fast depleting. The oil resources could be used for more important things than just manufacture plastic bags

In some countries, it is now required by law that stores provide shoppers with reusable bags. Bring Your Own Bag (BYOB) is an effort to reduce the use of plastic bags. Many people find it inconvenient to bring a bag with them when they go shopping. However, there are several benefits to using your own bag.

First, you can save money. Many grocery stores have started charging a nominal fee for customers who want a plastic bag. If you bring your own bag, you don't have to pay for one.

Second, you can help the reduce plastic use. Plastic bags are often not recycled and end up in landfills or the ocean. Third, you can help keep your town or city clean. Plastic bags can get caught in trees and bushes and cause an eyesore. Fourth, you can help keep food fresh.

That's a good start, but it's not enough. The real solution is to stop using plastic bags altogether and bring your own reusable cloth or eco bag when you go shopping. What's promising is that people are finding ways to manufacture shopping bags made from sustainable materials like bamboo, jute, hemp, and cotton. These bags not only look good, but they're also low-key helping reduce plastic pollution. So, the next time you go grocery shopping, make sure to bring your own sustainable shopping bag!

SHOP LOCAL AND SUPPORT LOCAL FARMERS

There are things we can do to reduce our reliance on plastics. One way to do this is to shop local and support local farmers. When you buy produce from a local farm, you're not only getting fresh, delicious food, but you're also reducing the amount of plastic pollution you create. That's because most local farmers don't use plastic bags to package their produce. Instead, they use baskets, paper, crates, or boxes.

So next time you go grocery shopping, try to buy your produce from a local farm whenever possible. You'll be doing your part to reduce plastic pollution while also getting some of the best food around.

BUY IN BULK

When most people think of ways to reduce their plastic footprint, they think about recycling. However, buying in bulk can be just as effective at reducing the amount of plastic waste produced each year.

Bulk buying is when shoppers purchase large quantities of a product, usually at a discounted price. This practice can help reduce the amount of packaging that is needed for each item. For example, if you need dishwashing liquid, you can purchase by the gallon instead of several smaller packages.

Not only does this save on packaging materials, but it also cuts down on transportation emissions since there is less need to ship multiple packages from different locations. Buying in bulk can be practical and economical, especially, if there are products that you use regularly and could get in larger quantities.

DRINK SUSTAINABLY

There are plenty of ways to drink coffee, tea, soda, and other beverages without contributing to the ever-growing plastic waste problem.

Single-use coffee pods and capsules are convenient and easy to use, but they come at a cost: the billions of disposable plastic pods used each year are neither recyclable nor compostable.

Most recycling centers are not willing to separate the plastic shell from the aluminum lid of the pods.

So, ditch the coffee pods and brew up a pot at home using your French press. But if you can't live without your precious Keurig and Nespresso, at least find compostable pods that are compatible with your coffee machines. This is so that the pods can be **recirculated as compost** for gardens and farms.

Bringing your own reusable cup to coffee shops is becoming more popular, and some shops like Starbucks even allow it. You can save money and help the environment by drinking your coffee this way. Reusable cups come in a variety of materials, so find the one that best suits your needs—as long it's not plastic. And while you're at it, ditch the disposable plastic stirrer as well.

If tea is more your thing, look for loose leaf varieties that come in refillable glass jars instead of plastic packaging. And when it comes to soda and other sugary drinks, try opting for seltzer water or homemade fruit juice instead.

Soda makers will also come in very handy if you want to make your fizzy drinks but don't want the plastic bottles. Making carbonated water and drinks at home using soda makers like SodaStream and Drinkmate is a more sustainable way to enjoy your favorite drinks.

By making small changes to the way you drink, you can help reduce waste and promote sustainability one non-plastic cup at a time.

LOOK FOR THE RECYCLING SYMBOL

We have no control of how stores package their produce. It's common for fruits, ready-meals, and meats to be wrapped in plastic or placed in plastic containers for sanitary reasons. More often than not, the packaging is not recyclable.

The next best thing that you can do is to check if the plastic containers are recyclable. Just look for the internationally recognizable recycling symbol of three chasing arrows with number code. This symbol indicates the type of plastic used. It gives you an idea if the plastic is safe for recycling.

- Polyethylene terephthalate (PETE 1) – PET bottles that are typically used for soft drinks and mineral water are generally safe to recycle.

- High-density polyethylene (HDPE 2) – These are plastic containers (e.g., milk jugs, oil bottles, and plastic bags) that are safe and easy to recycle. Only about 35% of HDPE plastic are recycled in the US. This is the safest type of plastic to use and recycle.

- Polyvinyl chloride (PVC 3) – Plastic trays, bubble foils, and clear plastic food wraps made from PVC release toxins. Most products using PVC use virgin materials in their construction. Only 1% of PVC products and materials are recycled. Although they can be repurposed, they are not recommended for reuse with food items.

- Low-density polyethylene (LDPE 4) – This type of plastic is used in grocery plastic bags, bread packaging, shrink wraps, and squeezable bottles. Although reusable, not all products made with LDPE are recyclable.

- Polypropylene (PP 5) – Polypropylene plastic is a strong and heat-resistant type of plastic. PP is typically used in potato chips bags, yogurt containers, and lining inside cereal boxes. Although PP is recyclable, only 3% of this type of plastic is being recycled in the US.

- Polystyrene (PS 6) – This type of plastic is used in meat trays, foam cups, takeout containers, clear egg cartons, and cutlery. Polystyrene can be recycled, but it is not always easy to do so. Some communities have curbside recycling programs for polystyrene products while others require that residents take them to special collection centers. This is why polystyrene products account for more than 35% of landfill waste in the US.

- Other Plastics (7) – This category refers to polycarbonates and other plastics. They are typically used in making baby bottles, sippy cups, and water cooler containers. Some plastics in this category may contain BPA (Bisphenol A), which is an endocrine disruptor. They are not safe for reuse and must be avoided.

Plastic recycling is an important component of the circular economy, as it decreases the amount of waste and plastic that ends up in landfills. Plastic recycling also lowers the cost of recycled plastic by removing the need for virgin raw materials like petroleum-based plastics to be made.

THE WORKPLACE

In response to the growing threat of plastic pollution, many people are now calling for a ban on plastic in the workplace. If your office provides disposable dishes or silverware, ask if they can switch to compostable or biodegradable materials instead.

While many companies are aware of the moral and ethical imperative to take action against plastic pollution, very few have made moves to eliminate or even reduce their use of plastic in the workplace. This is a problem because plastic is pervasive and it's often difficult to avoid using it when you're at work for at least eight hours of your waking life each day.

Even if your office doesn't have a recycling program, there are still things you can do to reduce your reliance on plastic in the workplace. One is to change your purchasing habits and only buy items that come in recyclable packaging. Better yet, bring your own lunch to work as well as containers, cups, and cutlery. It's an effective way to avoid buying foodstuffs wrapped in plastic packaging.

Another way is to encourage your co-workers to bring their own reusable cups, water bottles, and utensils instead of using disposable ones. However, not everyone will be receptive to the idea because it may be inconvenient for some people to do so. Start a conversation about how you can all work together to make the workplace more environmentally friendly.

Many companies have already started making changes to their operations. For example, Starbucks eliminated plastic straws from all of its stores, while Dunkin' Donuts ditched polystyrene foam cups. These changes may seem small, but they can make a big difference when adopted by large corporations.

As the public outcry for change grows louder, businesses are looking for ways to phase out single-use, disposable products from their supply chains. This shift away from convenience-oriented plastics also presents an opportunity for businesses to innovate and create new products that are more sustainable.

CHILDREN

It has been found that children are already exposed to plastic even before they are born through their mothers' exposure to it. A study published in Environment International in 2021 revealed that there are microplastic particles in human placentas. They are likely to have come from packaging materials, cosmetics, or paints, due to the colors of the particles. They were dyed in orange, pink, and red.

The chemicals in plastic can cross the placenta and affect the development of the fetus. This means that unborn children are potentially at risk for health problems later in life, including obesity, reproductive problems, and cancer. It is therefore important for pregnant women to take steps to reduce their exposure to plastics as much as possible. A change in diet and lifestyle may be required.

Although no one knows for sure what this means for the health of children in the long term, it is a cause for great concern and more research is needed to determine their potential health risks, especially whether their presence in the placenta can trigger the release of toxins or cause immune responses.

Children are especially vulnerable to the harmful effects of plastic because their bodies are still developing. They are exposed to plastic in a variety of ways. One way is through their food. Studies have found that BPA, a chemical found in some baby bottles, can leach into food and beverages. Another way children are exposed to plastic is through toys. Some toys are made with PVC, which contains phthalates. Phthalates are chemicals that can disrupt the endocrine system and cause health problems. Children can also be exposed to plastics through their skin. Some plastics contain additives that can be absorbed through the skin.

SWITCH TO CLOTH OR HYBRID DIAPERS

The average child will go through about 8,000 diapers before being potty trained. Most people don't think about what happens to disposable diapers after they're used. They're simply thrown away and forgotten about. The kind of plastic used in disposable diapers is not recyclable, meaning that it just sits in landfills and is not used for anything else.

There is now a movement to try and reduce this amount of waste by switching to cloth diapers or hybrid diapers.
There are many benefits to using cloth diapers over disposable ones. For one, they are much cheaper in the long run. Cloth diapers can be used and washed multiple times before being disposed of, while disposable diapers must be thrown away after each use. They are also better for the environment since disposable diapers take up to 500 years to decompose in a landfill.

Another benefit of cloth diapers is that they are more comfortable for babies. Disposable diapers can be quite stiff and uncomfortable, while cloth diapers are soft and gentle on baby's skin. They also allow babies to feel the wetness when they pee, which helps them learn to potty train earlier. Finally, cloth diapers are just cuter than disposable ones! There are so many fun prints and colors to choose from, and they can add a touch of personality to your baby's outfit. Use cloth diapers whenever possible. They may take a little more effort to wash, but they're better for the environment and your wallet.

A hybrid diaper, on the other hand, is a cloth diaper with a disposable insert. This means that you can get the benefits of both disposable and cloth diapers. One of the main benefits of using a hybrid diaper is that you can customize it to meet your needs. For example, if you are going on a long trip, you can use all disposable inserts so that you don't have to worry about laundry. If you are at home, you can use reusable inserts so that you can save money on diapers.

Another benefit of hybrid diapers is that they are easy to use. All you have to do is put the disposable insert into the cloth diaper and fasten it like normal.

Pampers and Huggies now offer hybrid diapers, but there are plenty of other options from smaller, independent brands.

USE PLASTIC-FREE BABY BOTTLES

When it comes to infant feeding, there are a lot of choices parents have to make. From the type of bottle to use to the kind of formula to buy, parents have a lot of decisions to make when it comes to their child's health.

One choice that some parents may not be aware of is whether or not to use plastic baby bottles. Many people assume that all baby bottles are made from plastic, but that is not the case. There are a number of different materials that baby bottles can be made from:

Glass baby bottles

Since there's growing concern that children are being exposed to too much plastic, some people are calling for a return to glass baby bottles. Glass baby bottles do not contain BPA. In fact, glass is a natural material that is inert and non-toxic. It does not leach chemicals into its contents, which makes it a safer choice for storing breast milk or formula. Glass is also easy to clean and does not harbor bacteria like plastic can. These are compelling reasons to switch from using plastic baby bottles to glass ones.

There are some potential drawbacks to using glass baby bottles. For one, they can be heavier and more difficult to clean than plastic bottles. Also, if they are dropped or broken, glass shards can pose a hazard to both the baby and caregivers. But these are just minor shortcomings. Some glass bottles now come with protective silicone sleeves so they don't break.

Glass baby bottles have a long history of safe use and are still considered to be one of the safest options available.

Stainless steel baby bottles

Stainless steel baby bottles are becoming an increasingly popular alternative to both glass and plastic. There are plenty of reasons why stainless steel is a good choice for baby bottles.

Stainless steel is non-toxic, meaning it's safe for your child to drink from. It doesn't leach chemicals or toxins into the milk like plastic can, and it's also free of BPA and phthalates. It's also hygienic and easy to clean—it doesn't have any tiny nooks or crannies that can be difficult to get bacteria out of.

Stainless steel baby bottles are often made with a vacuum insulation system that keeps the milk cool or warm on the inside and cold or hot on the outside. This is important because the temperature of your baby's food and drink can have a huge influence on how she feels. It's a durable, lightweight, and eco-friendly option.

Silicone baby bottles

Food grade silicone is a polymer made from silica, which is a lightweight, soft material that does not break. This material is often used in baby bottles because it is non-toxic and does not release chemicals into the food or beverage. In addition, silicone is easy to clean and does not hold onto bacteria like some other materials can.

Silicone baby bottles are the perfect choice for parents looking for a safe and flexible bottle that is easy for little ones to hold. Silicone is a soft and pliable material, which makes these bottles squishy and easy to grip.

USE ALTERNATIVES TO PLASTIC PACIFIERS

Pacifiers and dummies have been around for a long time, but with the recent concerns about the use of plastic in these items, parents are looking for alternatives. Here are some of the best options:

Babies can suck on a rubber nipple or a piece of cloth to soothe themselves. This is a great option for parents who want to avoid using plastic. If you do choose to use a pacifier or dummy, there are some made from latex or silicone that are safer than those made from plastic.

An example of an environmentally friendly alternative to traditional pacifiers is HEVEA pacifiers. They are made from 100% natural rubber latex and are free of BPA, PVC, phthalates, and artificial colors. They come in a variety of shapes and sizes to fit your child's mouth, and the nipples are soft and flexible.

There are some pacifiers and dummies available in the market that claim to be "natural," but they are actually made from a mix of bamboo and polypropylene. So, be sure to check the material before purchasing.

BUY TOYS THAT ARE BUILT TO LAST AND REUSABLE

Unbeknownst to many, the toy industry is the most plastic-intensive industry in the world. About 90% of the toys available in the market are made of some form plastic. Aside the plastic components, the toys may also contain harmful chemicals like phthalates.

Over 80 percent of these toys often end up in landfills and contribute to the growing problem of plastic pollution. Aside from contributing to plastic pollution, these toys can also be a health risk to children. When they chew on plastic toys, they can ingest the chemicals or choke on the small pieces.

Researchers are now urging parents to be more mindful of the types of toys they buy for their children and to recycle or reuse old toys whenever possible.

Unfortunately, most recycling facilities don't recycle toys because it is too costly to break them down into their individual pieces and process them. This is especially true for toys made of plastic, which can be difficult to recycle because they tend to be very brittle.

There are a few recycling facilities that do recycle plastic toys, but the process is not always efficient. For example, the facility might only recycle certain types of plastic toys, or they might only accept certain colors of plastic. In addition, the process often requires cleaning the toy parts before they can be recycled, which can add additional time and cost to the overall process.

Municipal solid waste services in the United States would need to invest in new equipment and hire additional staff in order to recycle toys, and that investment would not be worth it when most toys end up in a landfill anyway.

The average American child receives more than 70 new toys a year worth over $6,500. Most of these toys are forgotten, broken, or thrown away in just a short time. The sheer number of toys and playthings that are available on the market makes it easy for children to own vast collections. These toys can end up in the trash as kids outgrow them.

The good news is that a lot of parents repurpose the toys or pass them down to younger kids. If you are going this route, make sure that you are handing down age-appropriate toys to your kids. Furthermore, the toys should not have significant wear and tear. Old toys can fall apart and small kids can put small parts in their mouths and may choke on them.

Popular toy brand LEGO contributes to global plastic pollution to the tune of 100,000 tons of plastic each year, which is equivalent to 110 billion LEGO bricks. To remedy this and avoid backlash, LEGO is looking to sugarcane as a way to make its LEGO pieces more environmentally friendly.

The sugarcane will be used to create a bioplastic that is made from plant-based materials rather than traditional plastics, which are made from oil—acrylonitrile-butadiene-styrene (ABS) to be precise. LEGO has been working on this project for several years and plans to have the new pieces available in 2030. Until then, consider using wooden blocks for your kid's eco-friendly enjoyment.

That may be a long way to go, but this shift away from traditional plastics is part of a larger trend towards more environmentally friendly materials in the toy industry. While there are some concerns about the environmental impact of sugarcane cultivation, LEGO believes that this is still a more sustainable option than using traditional plastics.

Until toy companies find sustainable ways to manufacture toys, you can take action and find eco-friendly ways for your children to enjoy toys safely. A great option is to shop at a consignment store or second-hand store. You can find used toys that are still in great condition, and you're helping to reduce waste by not buying new toys.

Another option is to buy wooden toys or organic cotton dolls. These types of toys are made from sustainable materials and they won't end up in a landfill when your child outgrows them. You can also make homemade playdough using ingredients you can find at home.

HOST ECO-FRIENDLY CHILDREN'S PARTIES

Children's birthday parties can be a lot of fun, but what many people don't know is that they're also a major source of plastic waste. When organizing a children's party, many parents turn to plastic items because they are convenient.

Plastic tablecloths and napkins can be easily wiped clean, and plastic plates and cups can be thrown away after the party. This eliminates the need to wash dishes or worry about spills. Additionally, using plastic decorations is a quick and easy way to add color and excitement to the party space. By choosing plastic items, parents can focus on enjoying the celebration with their children rather than worrying about cleanup.

Just think about all the decorations, balloons, glitter, goodie bags, party plates, cups, and utensils that are used. Most of these items are made out of plastic and they all end up in the landfill after the party is over.

With proper planning and reasonable time for preparation, you can have a sustainable children's party with zero plastic.

- **Decorations can be made with natural materials that can be reused or recycled.** You can use paper products that can be repurposed, such as old magazines, maps, posters, or postcards. You can also make origami flowers or insects out of colorful paper to add a touch of whimsy to the party decorations. You can also use paper streamers and banners, which can be easily recycled after the party is over.

- **Ditch the traditional glitter and go for an eco-friendly alternative**. Biodegradable glitter is made from plant-based materials like corn starch and sugarcane. It comes in a variety of colors and can be used to decorate cards, invitations, goody bags, and even cake pops. Another option is edible glitter. This type of glitter is made from edible materials like sugar, corn starch, and food coloring. It can be sprinkled on top of cakes, cupcakes, and other desserts. Not only does it look pretty, but it also adds a delicious flavor.

- **Use virtual invites.** If you want RSVP tracking, you can use electronic invitation services like Greenvelope, Punchbowl, or Evite. To create your virtual invite, start by deciding on a theme. Then, choose a color scheme and design your invitation around that. You can use photos or animation software to create an engaging invite that will grab the kids' attention. Once you've created your invite, send it to your guests online via email or text message. Be sure to include all the pertinent information, such as the date, time, and location of the party. You can also include a map or directions if needed. The kids can view them on PCs, phones, tablets, or mobile devices.

- **Use compostable plates, cups, straws, and utensils.** Compostable tableware is made from materials like corn starch, sugarcane bagasse, or bamboo fiber. So, when you're finished with them, you can simply throw them in the compost bin and they will break down naturally.

- **Give away eco-friendly party favors.** Trinkets, art supplies, homemade treats, books, painted shirts (that the kids made during the party), homemade playdough, and temporary tattoos made from vegetable ink are some of your options to put in the goodie bags.

PETS

The number of dog poop bags disposed of every year is estimated at 415 billion, which is equivalent to about 1.23 million tons of dog poop bags. This accounts for 0.6 percent of the total global plastic waste generation. It may seem like it's only a small fraction of plastic waste, but it's considered a non-negligible source of plastic pollution.

In the United States alone, there are about 70 million households that own at least one dog. That means there is a lot of poop to pick up! This is why dog poop bags have become an indispensable product for pet owners.

But this convenience comes with a price. The chemical composition of dog poop bags is largely polyethylene, the prevailing type of polymer found in the environment as a result of plastic waste disposal. Furthermore, they may contain pathogens, such as *Salmonella*, *Clostridium perfringens*, and *Campylobacter jejuni*, which have the potential to spread disease.

This underscores the importance of proper disposal of dog poop bags, as even a single bag that is not properly disposed of can contaminate water sources and lead to the spread of diseases not just to animals but humans as well. Hence, dog poop bags eventually become toxic pollutants, which result in adverse biological and environmental effects.

On average, a dog owner uses more than 900 dog poop bags annually. This can quickly add up, especially with the rising number of dog owners worldwide. It will continue to go on an upward trend unless alternative materials are used to at least disrupt the consumption pattern of plastic-based dog poop bags.

USE ALTERNATIVES TO PLASTIC DOG POOP BAGS

Picking up dog poop is a necessary evil for all dog owners, but it doesn't have to be with a plastic bag. There are only a few options when it comes to alternatives to plastic dog poop bags. Although they are far from perfect, they can help reduce plastic pollution in small but significant ways.

- **Biodegradable and Compostable Dog Poop Bags** – These bags degrade faster compared to their synthetic counterparts. Depending on the brand and the materials used, it can take anywhere from 3 to 6 months to degrade.

- **Paper Dog Poop Bags** – Paper is a great alternative to plastic poop bags and it's an eco-friendly way to clean up after your dogs. It may not be as durable as plastic, but it can get the job done. Pooch Paper is an example of a product that can be used to scoop up dog waste. The paper is lined with grease-resistant coating made from corn to prevent leakage.

COMMUNITY

While combating plastic pollution requires a concerted global effort, there are things that individuals can do to reduce their own contribution to the problem. One easy way to do this is to make a conscious effort to reduce consumption of disposable plastics, such as straws, bags, and water bottles.

Fighting plastic pollution can start at the individual level but community initiatives help move the needle towards the ultimate goal. Because of the internet and other technologies we have at our disposal, organizing campaigns on a local, national, and international level has never been easier, stronger, and more impactful.

There are now more community initiatives to fight plastic pollution than ever before. This is a good thing, because it will take a combined effort to make the necessary changes to stop the flow of plastic into our oceans. But we also need to remember that organizing on a community level has never been stronger. We need to use this power to push for change and make sure our voices are heard.

As they say, there's strength in numbers and in collective good will. A group of people passionate about the environment can band together and make a difference.

Here are some ways for community members to help fight plastic pollution.

- **Recycling** is one of the most important steps community members can take to reduce the amount of plastic waste at the local level. Local governments and private companies offer recycling services for a variety of materials, including plastic.

- **Beach cleanups** are another way to help remove plastics and other debris from the environment. Coastal communities and organizations often host cleanup events, which participants can find online or through word-of-mouth.

- Individuals can also **write to their local representatives** about the need for stricter regulations on single-use plastics. Urging policymakers to implement legislation that would ban or tax products like plastic straws, bags, and bottles can help reduce the amount of waste produced each year.

- One way to reduce plastic waste is to **encourage the youth to lead community efforts**. Youth groups are often very enthusiastic about making a difference in their communities and are eager to learn about ways they can help. They can be a powerful force for change and can inspire others to take action as well.

- **Help raise awareness** about the growing problem of plastic pollution by using social media. Share information about plastic pollution, post photos and videos of its harmful effects to health and environment, and use hashtags like #plasticpollution and #saynotoplastic.

You can also tag influential people and organizations who are working to combat plastic pollution. For example, @natgeo, @world_wildlife, and @greenpeace. By raising awareness on social media, we can all play a part in solving the problem of plastic pollution.

We need to rethink our approach to plastic waste and find ways to reduce or eliminate its use altogether. We can start by making changes at the individual level and becoming more conscious of the amount of plastic we use on a daily basis. We can also advocate for policy changes at the local, state, and federal levels. It's time for us to take action and protect our communities and our planet from the growing threat of plastic pollution.

THE DARK SIDE OF RECYCLING

Recycling is the last resort for most plastic waste. For products to be recycled, they must be collected and processed at a recycling facility. The recycling process begins by sorting the products into different categories based on material type. The products are then cleaned and shredded or chopped into small pieces before they are melted down and formed into new products.

By recycling plastics, we are able to reduce the amount of waste that goes into our landfills and ultimately cut down our plastic pollution. When we recycle, we also reduce the use of virgin plastics and use less energy compared to creating products from scratch. Thus, recycling helps us conserve depleting resources like water, oil, and energy.

But according to the Environmental Protection Agency, only about 8 percent of plastic was recycled in the United States in 2018. That number pales in comparison to the recycling rate of paper (68 percent), glass (31 percent) or aluminum (35 percent), which suggests that recycling plastic isn't as efficient as we thought.

There are several reasons for this low recycling rate:

- **Plastic is difficult to recycle.** It can't be melted down and reformed like metal can, so it has to be chopped into small pieces and cleaned before it can be used again. This process is expensive and time-consuming, which means that most recyclers don't bother with plastic.

- **Not all plastics are created equal.** Not all types of plastics can be melted down and made into new products right away. More often than not, the plastic content has to be separated from other materials before it can be recycled.

  Some types of plastic are easier to recycle than others. For example, polyethylene terephthalate (PET), which is used in many beverage bottles, is easy to recycle because it can be melted down and turned back into bottles or other products made from PET. Products made from polyvinyl chloride (PVC), on other hand, contain different additives and other components. So, when they are fed to a mechanical recycler or grinder, the composition of the resulting granules (recyclate) is unpredictable and of low-quality. They are considered to have lower economic value.

Post-consumer plastic waste with PVC has to undergo further sorting and cleaning, which adds to the cost of the recycling process. That's why not many recycling centers handle recycling PVCs.

- **Plastic products are not designed with recycling in mind.** Too often, plastic products are designed for one-time use and not meant for recycling. This kind of thinking limits recycling efforts. That's why manufacturers must consider recycling issues at the design stage. This means designing products that can easily be broken down and recycled. It also means using less plastic overall, which can help reduce environmental pollution.

- **Lack of collaboration among stakeholders.** In order to effect real change, it takes a collaborative effort from the entire product chain to improve recycling rates—from the raw material suppliers to manufacturers to end user.

  Manufacturers should design plastic products that make it easier for consumers to recycle their products. And suppliers must prove a steady supply of recycled plastic raw materials so that manufacturers can continue to make innovative products

  In order to increase the use of recycled plastics, it is crucial to develop a more reliable supply chain for these materials. This will require investment in new recycling infrastructure as well as partnerships between public and private entities.

  By working together, we can create a sustainable system for recycling plastic that will benefit both the environment and the economy.

- **Lack of public education on proper recycling.** Many people do not know how to properly clean and prepare plastic waste for recycling. Many municipalities do not have the resources necessary to educate residents about recycling. As a result, much of the plastic waste that could be recycled ends up being disposed of in landfills.

  This issue can be addressed by increasing public education campaigns about recycling, and by providing more resources to municipalities so they can educate residents about recycling.

FAULTY RECYCLING SYSTEM IN THE UNITED STATES

The benefits of recycling are clear. It helps to reduce pollution and conserve resources. It also creates jobs in the recycling industry. Recycling facilities are an important part of our economy and our environment. But the sad truth is that recycling is far from perfect.

The United States has more than 630 materials recycling facilities that process more than 100,000 tons of recyclables per day. Only less than 10 percent of discarded plastics make it to the recycling stream. About 15 percent is burned in waste-to-energy facilities and 75 percent is dumped in landfills. This means that the US lags behind European Union (39 percent) and China (22 percent) when it comes to recycling. It also shows that the recycling system in the US is not as efficient as other countries.

Although recycling facilities exist all over the country, the recycling system in the United States is faulty and inefficient. The United States recycles using a single-stream recycling system. This means that all recyclable materials are placed in the same container for collection, instead of being sorted into different types of recyclables.

The benefits of using a single-stream recycling system are that it is easier for people to recycle, and it is more efficient for the recycling trucks to collect the materials. The downside is that there is more contamination in the recycled materials, which can decrease the quality of the recycled products. Furthermore, the mixed materials are difficult and expensive to sort and clean at recycling facilities. In many cases, recycled plastic can't be used to create new products because it doesn't meet quality standards.

What this tells us is that the United States faces a major obstacle—the lack of efficient and robust waste infrastructure. In other words, the US does not have the ability to recycle most of its plastic waste. Plus, there is really no secondary end market for recycled products in the country. This is the reason why the US has been exporting more than half of its plastic waste to China, a country with the capability to process plastic waste and has the market for recycled products.

However, China banned the importation of plastic waste in 2018. Once the ban is fully implemented, the estimated plastic waste that will be displaced is 111 million metric tons. This ban is likely to have a devastating impact on the recycling industry in the United States. The US can either handle the problem domestically or export to another country. Plastic waste is already difficult to recycle, and now there is nowhere to send it to.

Let's face it, the recycling system in the United States is broken, but there's also the nefarious side of the story where recycling is said to be just a devious strategy of the plastic industry to continue producing plastic products limitlessly.

In the Frontline PBS documentary, Plastic Wars, an internal document from the Society of the Plastics Industry Inc revealed the following:

> "The techniques of cleaning and separating the mixed plastics in major kinds of resins has not been developed for large scale economic application."

"There are no effective market mechanisms for trade in contaminated, mixed plastics."

"There's serious doubt that it can ever be made viable on an economic basis."

This puts a lot of pressure for the government, manufacturers, and suppliers to find new solutions to recycle plastic products. One potential solution to this problem is to invest in new waste infrastructure, including new recycling facilities that could process more recyclable materials. Another solution is to create a stronger secondary market for recycled materials in the United States.

And if recycling is not the real solution for now, then companies must find a way to make products that function and perform like plastic but could break down fast.

The good news is that there are companies that rise to the occasion. Terravive is one of them. The company makes compostable and ocean-degradable consumer products—cups, bags, takeout containers, cutlery, straws, bowls, and plates. These products are made from plant materials that break down in months, not centuries. Terravive aims to accelerate the transition to a circular economy.

If more companies follow suit, plastic production will be significantly reduced. And if the recycling system is improved, then plastic waste can be manageable.

RECYCLING THAT WORKS

The act of recycling is not a new concept, but the way society recycles has changed over time. In the early days of recycling, people would recycle items such as glass and aluminum cans because those items were easy to recycle. They could be sold to companies that would recycle them into new products.

Because there's economies of scale, recycling companies are able to process waste at a lower per-unit cost, which can lead to increased profits and competitiveness. This can be achieved through the use of specialized equipment, division of labor, and the ability to purchase raw materials in bulk.

Many communities have also found that there are cost savings associated with recycling programs. These savings come from two primary sources: reduced waste disposal costs and the sale of recyclable materials. As recycling became more popular, society began to recycle items for environmental reasons, not financial reasons.

Despite society's good intentions, recycling can be difficult to do effectively. In some cases, it can be more expensive to recycle an item than it is to simply throw it away, like in the case of single-use plastics. Additionally, not all plastic materials can be recycled. Even with these challenges, recycling can still work if everyone does their part.

To find the most feasible solution for recycling plastic products, it's important to understand what the options are.

4 MAIN RECYCLING MECHANISMS FOR THERMOPLASTICS

1. Primary Recycling (Closed Loop)

In a primary recycling process, the recycled material is used to make identical products. With a closed loop, the recycled material can be used in other products but the physical and chemical state of the plastic remains unchanged. The downside to this is the limited number of cycles. This means that the plastic product has a limited life cycle due to wear and tear.

2. Secondary Recycling (Mechanical)

The process of recycling plastics begins by breaking down the large pieces of used plastic into smaller fragments. These fragments are then heated until they liquefy. The molten plastic is poured into a mold, where it cools and hardens into the desired shape. This process is known as secondary recycling, and it allows us to reuse old plastic products to create new ones.

One benefit of secondary recycling is that it reduces the amount of plastic that ends up in landfills. By reusing old plastic products, we can reduce the amount of new plastic that needs to be produced. Secondary recycling also helps to conserve energy and resources.

3. Feedstock Recycling (Chemical)

This type of recycling involves breaking down the polymers into smaller units, which are then fed back into the production cycle so that they can be used as raw materials to make new plastic products.

The downside is that chemical recycling can be costly. Not all recycling facilities do feedstock recycling due to the prohibitive cost and complex processing. Plus, its true impact on the environment is still under debate.

4. Quaternary Recycling (Incineration)

This type of recycling involves the incineration of plastics to produce energy that can be used to generate electricity or heat. The process of incineration converts the plastic into gas, which is then burned to create heat. The heat is used to produce steam, which in turn powers turbines that generate electricity.

Although the burning of plastic is considered one of the most efficient ways to create energy from waste, it's not eco-friendly. The biggest problem with incinerating plastic waste is that it releases toxic pollutants into the air. These pollutants can cause respiratory problems and other health issues. They can also contaminate water supplies and harm wildlife.

In addition, incinerating plastic waste creates large amounts of greenhouse gases, which contribute to climate change. The emissions from just one incinerator can be equivalent to the emissions from thousands of cars.

Therefore, incinerating plastic waste is not a sustainable or eco-friendly solution to the problem of plastic pollution. There are better ways to recycle plastic waste that don't have these destructive effects.

Clearly, every option has its pros and cons, but it would be foolish to believe that we can recycle our way out of the plastic predicament we are in. But what can be done in the community and individual level to make recycling efficient even at a smaller scale?

SMALL WINS: DEPOSIT ON PLASTIC BOTTLES

In an effort to reduce the amount of waste that goes into landfills, some states have implemented bottle bill or container deposit return law. These laws require that a certain percentage of the price of a beverage container is refunded to the consumer when the container is returned to a designated redemption center.

Bottle bill has been shown to reduce litter and increase recycling rates, and many local governments support their implementation—because it simply works! This is largely because deposits create a financial incentive for people to recycle their plastic bottles and cans. In states without bottle bills, there is no incentive to return containers, so most people simply toss them in the trash. With a deposit, people are more likely to recycle their containers because they can get their money back.

Container-deposit legislation achieves the following:

- Encourages recycling ad reduces plastic bottle litter along highways, in rivers and lakes, and public properties.

- Reduces the number of plastic beverage containers that need to be manufactured, which in turn, conserves energy, water, virgin plastic materials, and other resources.

- Reduces greenhouse gas emissions.

- Extends the usable lifespan of landfills as there is a reduction in the amount of plastic waste.

- Complements curbside recycling programs.

- Creates a more sustainable circular economy and also creates jobs in the recycling industry.

Currently, bottle bill is implemented in 10 states in the United States. The following states have very high return rate because of the legislation.

1. California (62%)
2. Connecticut (44%)
3. Hawaii (72%)
4. Iowa (65%)
5. Maine (84%)
6. Massachusetts (43%)
7. Michigan (89%)
8. New York (64%)
9. Oregon (86%)
10. Vermont (77%)

TERRACYCLE: STEPPING UP TO ELIMINATE THE IDEA OF WASTE

Despite the shortcomings of recycling, the global recycling market is expected to grow by $14.74 billion by 2024. This is an opportunity for companies to incorporate the use of high-quality recycled plastic into the products they produce. Furthermore, recycling facilities can benefit from enhancing the quality of the recycled plastic they produce.

Many companies are seeing the economic and environmental impact, but only a few are stepping up their game. One of them is TerraCycle and it's on a mission to eliminate the idea of waste through innovation and partnership. Clearly, it's not some two-bit curbside recycler.

The New Jersey-based company has developed ground-breaking new ways to recycle everything from cigarette butts to baby food pouches. One of TerraCycle's effective programs is its Zero Waste Box. These boxes are designed to collect hard-to-recycle items like candy wrappers and shampoo bottles. Once the box is filled up, the company sends a team to pick it up and recycle the contents.

Researchers at TerraCycle analyze the materials to determine the right way to process them into something new. For example, they may find that certain materials can be recycled into plastic pellets that can be used to make new products. This research and development team is always looking for ways to improve recycling and reduce waste.

The recycling process begins by sorting the materials into different categories based on their physical and chemical properties. This is done using a variety of technologies, including manual sorting, magnetic, optical sorters, and air jets, among others.

TerraCycle also offers a free recycling program for schools and non-profit organizations. The program allows schools and organization to recycle everything from used markers to yogurt cups. In addition, TerraCycle donates money to the school for every pound of recyclable material collected.

Thanks to companies like TerraCycle, it is becoming easier than ever to recycle unwanted items. Best of all, it's not limited to just plastics. When TerraCycle said that it wanted to eliminate the idea of wastes, the company meant they #RecycleEverything.

BRIGHTMARK: A BRIGHT SPOT IN RECYCLING

Brightmark, a San Francisco-based waste solution company, is changing the way we think about organic waste. Not only are they turning it into renewable natural gas, but they're also finding innovative ways to renew plastics through science.

This is a company that is committed to sustainability through cutting-edge technology and powerful partnerships. With Brightmark at the forefront of this industry, we can be confident that we're moving in the right direction when it comes to preserving our planet.

Brightmark turns plastic waste into fuel and other products. By using technology that can recycle any kind of plastic, including single-use items like water bottles and straws, the company is helping reduce the amount of plastic that ends up in landfills and oceans, while also creating new products and generating jobs.

The company believes that the key to solving both the plastic crisis and greenhouse gas emissions lies in circularity. More specifically, investing in new technologies that will create a closed-loop economy in which products are reused and recycled rather than ending up in landfills or incinerators. Simply put, the company takes our trash and creates new products from it. A very ambitious undertaking but they're making it work at a global scale.

Brightmark is also working to develop markets for recycled materials, which will make it more economical to recycle plastics and other materials rather than produce new products from virgin materials. If Brightmark's vision for a circular economy becomes a reality, it could have a major impact on the environment and the global economy.

CHAPTER 6: NEUTRALIZE PLASTIC POLLUTION IMPACT

In today's society, it is nearly impossible to avoid plastic products. The ubiquity of disposable plastics in our everyday lives—from water bottles and shopping bags to straws and cutlery—means that most of us contribute daily to the problem. Plastic pollution is one of the most pressing environmental issues of our time, and it's only going to get worse unless we take action.

There are many ways we can reduce our individual plastic footprint. We can start by having the willpower to refuse single-use plastics whenever possible, recycle what we can't avoid using, and support organizations that are working to fight plastic pollution.

Volunteering for these organizations is a great way to make a difference, help raise awareness about this critical issue, and neutralize the impact of plastic pollution.

- **Volunteer** with an organization that focuses on cleaning up beaches, rivers, and lakes. There are many great organizations out there that need volunteers to help clean up our planet. Find one that aligns with your values and passions and offer your time and energy!

- **Sign up** for a charity that is working to reduce plastic pollution. If you are unable to volunteer your time, you can make a donation.

- **Get involved** in activism to promote change. Speak out against corporations, governments, and personalities that allow plastic pollution to persist. Join a movement or start your own to create awareness and inspire change.

- **Take action** to reduce your plastic consumption. Don't use plastic straws, cutlery, or water bottles. Use cloth bags when shopping. Bring your own mug to the coffee shop and ask for a refill. Reduce what you buy, recycle or compost what you can, and give the rest away!

THE PLASTIC-FREE MOVEMENT

The plastic-free movement is a global effort to reduce the amount of plastic waste that is produced and disposed of each year. It encourages people to get involved in advocacy activities that raise awareness about the dangers of plastic pollution and find sustainable solutions to this global problem.

In the fight against plastic pollution, consumers are often blamed for the waste problem. After all, it is our reliance on disposable plastics that has created the mountains of waste we see today. For the longest time, the industry has maintained that plastic pollution is the result of poor waste management and littering. But this framing obscures the true extent of the problem and diverts attention from the root causes of plastic pollution.

The plastic-free movement, made up of grassroots and environmental organizations, is challenging this by highlighting the impacts of plastics at every stage of their life cycle. As the movement gains traction, it becomes increasingly clear that reducing plastic consumption is only one part of the solution. The real challenge lies in tackling the systemic problem at source.

BREAK FREE FROM PLASTIC (BFFP)

Break Free From Plastic is an 11,000-strong movement made up of organizations and people from all walks of life who are coming together to demand change—for corporations to stop producing single-use plastics, for governments to put in place policies that reduce plastic waste, and for everyone else to do their part in reducing their reliance on plastic.

In an effort to better understand the landscape of plastic pollution, BFFP conducts brand audits at various locations around the world. The goal is to identify the companies responsible for producing and selling products with the most plastic waste.

The movement's global brand audit report, released in 2018, found that a shocking number of companies are producing and selling products that contribute to plastic pollution. Coca-Cola was identified as the top polluter, with PepsiCo and Nestlé close behind. The report confirms what we've long suspected—big brands are responsible for most of the plastic pollution.

By conducting brand audits, BFFP is exposing the real actors behind the plastic crisis we are experiencing now and debunking the myth perpetrated by the industry that consumers and waste management systems are to blame—when in fact, the industry has been the main culprit all along.

The findings are significant because they show which companies need to be targeted for change. By identifying and exposing the biggest polluters, BFFP can work to hold these corporations accountable and push them towards more sustainable practices.

PLASTIC POLLUTION COALITION (PPC)

The Plastic Pollution Coalition is a global alliance of individuals, organizations, businesses, and governments working together to educate people about the dangers of plastic pollution and inspire action to reduce it.

Established in 2009, PPC is a non-profit organization that promotes solutions that can help reverse the devastating effects of plastic pollution. The PPC has developed a number of resources and an online guide on how to live life without disposable plastic, with the ultimate goal of reducing plastic footprint across different settings and situations.

The PPC's mission is to end the global epidemic of plastic pollution through public education, grassroots activism, and engagement with businesses and governments.

PPC has a controversial stance on recycling plastic, arguing that it's actually a bad option. The coalition points to the environmental impact of producing new plastic from recycled material, as it takes more energy to recycle plastic than it does to simply produce new plastic from oil. This increased energy use creates more greenhouse gas emissions, which contributes to climate change.

In order to combat the plastic pollution crisis, PPC has identified changing legal structures and producer responsibility as key priorities. One of PPC's primary goals is to shift the focus from individual responsibility for recycling to producer responsibility. This means holding companies accountable for the products they produce and ensuring that those products are designed and manufactured in a way that minimizes waste. PPC also wants to see laws changed so that producers are responsible for cleaning up their products once they've been discarded. This would help reduce the amount of plastic pollution.

5 GYRES INSTITUTE

Another group working to combat plastic pollution is 5 Gyres, an organization that conducts scientific research on ocean plastics. It has been at the forefront of research and public education on the global issue of plastic pollution.

5 Gyres was instrumental in getting microbeads–tiny pieces of plastic found in personal care products–banned in the United States through the Microbeads Free Waters Act of 2015. The law, which took effect on July 17, 2017, bans the production, packaging, and distribution of rinse-off cosmetics and personal care products that contain microbeads.

Through the Plastics BAN (Better Alternatives Now) initiative, 5 Gyres calls for a ban on the production and use of all single-use plastics and suggests eco-friendly and viable alternatives. One of the biggest challenges facing the Plastics BAN is persuading people to switch to reusable alternatives.

Using data from scientific reports and their own expeditions, the organization has shown that the amount of plastic in our oceans is far greater than previously thought. This knowledge is helping to change the way people think about their use of plastics and convince them to take action against plastic pollution.

LIVING LANDS & WATERS (LL&W)

Led by its founder Chad Pregracke, Living Lands & Waters has been the driving force in river cleanup since 1998. There is simply no other organization like it in the world. Their crews are made up of experienced commercial fishermen, outdoor enthusiasts, and volunteers who have a true passion for preserving our nation's waterways.

What separates Living Lands & Waters from other cleanup organizations is their "industrial strength approach." They have the resources and manpower to clean up even the most heavily polluted areas. From major rivers and lakes to small streams and creeks, Living Lands & Waters has a proven track record of success, with over 12 million pounds of trash removed and 1.8 million trees planted to date.

With massive cleanup projects in Illinois and other parts of the country, LL&W is working towards restoring rivers and areas to their natural state and creating new opportunities for wildlife to thrive in better ecosystems.

The Living Lands & Waters team is also dedicated to educating others about the importance of keeping our waterways clean. They hold free public workshops throughout the year and provide education materials on their website.

4OCEAN

4ocean is a company that was created with a vision to help clean up the world's oceans. They do this by removing plastic and other debris from the water, and by raising awareness about the issue of ocean pollution. 4ocean also partners with organizations that are dedicated to protecting the ocean.

4ocean is on a mission to clean up the world's oceans. With a fleet of vessels and river boom systems operated by full-time captains and crew, 4ocean is able to design a custom recovery system that can be deployed in both deep and shallow water. This system allows the crew to collect plastic from the ocean's surface, as well as its floor. This results in the recovery of tons of plastic debris from coastal areas.

Massive cleanup operations in Florida, Hawaii, Indonesia, Haiti, Guatemala, and other areas resulted in more than 24 million pounds of trash being recovered from rivers, oceans, coastlines, and waterways.

As a for-profit organization with a heart for the planet, 4ocean has created a line of eco-friendly alternatives to single-use plastics. The company also sells apparel, bracelets, accessories, and cleanup gear on their website. Proceeds from the sales of these items go towards funding ocean cleanup initiatives.

THE OCEAN CLEANUP

The Ocean Cleanup, a Dutch non-profit organization founded in 2013 by Boyan Slat, is developing and scaling technologies to rid the world's oceans of plastic. The group has designed a system of large floating barriers that act as a giant filter, catching plastic debris while allowing fish and ocean animals to pass underneath.

The technology used in the cleanup is designed to passively intercept and extract floating debris from the ocean surface (also called legacy plastic). The idea is to turn off the tap and mop the floor using a network of U-shaped booms anchored to the seabed with weighted screens hanging below the surface to capture plastics and other debris. Once a screen has filled with debris, it is brought to the surface and emptied onto a barge for recycling.

The first deployment took place in the Great Pacific Garbage Patch, located halfway between Hawaii and California. If the cleanup project is successful, it could be deployed worldwide to help clean up the estimated 8 million tons of plastic that enter the ocean each year.

The Ocean Cleanup plans to remove 90% of floating ocean plastic by the year 2040. Although the goal is ambitious, the organization believes it is achievable through concerted global effort. And when the world's oceans are clean, the organization will be more than happy to put itself out of business.

GREENPEACE

Greenpeace is an international non-governmental organization with the goal of protecting the planet and promoting peace through global campaigns. It was founded in 1971 by Canadian journalists Irving Stowe and Dorothy Stowe, Paul Cote, and French diver Jean-Luc Van Den Heede who were frustrated with the lack of leadership in the environmental movement. Greenpeace has offices in over 55 countries and relies on a global network of volunteers to achieve its goals.

Greenpeace is best known for its activist campaigns targeting whaling, nuclear weapons, seal hunting, commercial fishing, deforestation, and plastic pollution. The group has also been involved in protests against genetic engineering and climate change. Greenpeace relies heavily on grassroots activism to achieve its goals; it has been criticized for being anti-corporate and overly reliant on sensationalism to gain media attention.

As part of its campaign to pressure companies to come up with real and innovative solutions to tackle plastic pollution, Greenpeace mounted the #ReuseRevolution campaign, which is a call for companies to take action and invest in technologies and resources to reuse sustainable materials and end the throwaway culture.

PLASTIC SOUP FOUNDATION

This organization is on a mission to reduce the amount of plastic soup in the world's oceans. The Plastic Soup Foundation has been very successful in raising awareness about the dangers of plastic pollution by disseminating information and scientific results to individuals and communities using traditional and social media channels.

Through its programs, the organization encourages people to take steps to reduce their plastic consumption, help clean up the environment, and limit their exposure to plastics. Some of the projects that the foundation is involved in include microplastic removal and clean-ups using new techniques and state-of-the-art technology for clearing rivers and sand.

By gaining an observer status in the United Nations Environment Programme, the Plastic Soup Foundation is able to amplify its message to get the government, the plastic industry, the big corporations, and the media to make better decisions and create real solutions to solve the plastic soup problem.

PRECIOUS PLASTIC

The main goal of Precious Plastic is to reduce plastic pollution by teaching people to create new products from plastic waste. It introduces a global alternative recycling system where people, machines, platforms, and creative ideas work together to fix the plastic problem in small but significant ways.

Precious Plastic is essentially an open source recycling project where all source materials, codes, and information are accessible by everyone. A starter kit is available for download to anyone who wants to start their recycling spaces.

The system is made up of a series of small, modular machines that can be used to recycle plastic waste into new products. The machines are designed to be easy to use and can be set up in any location.

The shredder breaks down large pieces of plastic into small pieces, the washer cleans the plastic, the granulator turns the small pieces of plastic into pellets, the injection molder forms new products from the pellets, and the extruder melts down old products and forms them into new ones.

Through the power of community, collaboration, and social media, knowledge can be communicated quickly and efficiently, making the system conducive for finding solutions and ideas to help fight plastic pollution.

PLASTIC BANK

Plastic Bank is on a mission to stop ocean plastic by promoting ethical recycling and empowering people to become Ocean Stewards. The organization believes that ocean plastic waste is not unstoppable. Members and supporters focus on collection and cleanup initiatives in vulnerable coastal areas around the world. The goal is to stop the plastic waste before they reach the ocean.

Part of Plastic Bank's program is to support affected communities by providing them with jobs as collectors. This not only helps clean the environment, but also helps alleviate poverty by giving members of the community the opportunity to earn and build better lives under the program.

Through its partnership with individuals, small businesses, and large enterprises, Plastic Bank is able to reduce plastic waste and turn them into Social Plastic. This plastic is reprocessed, transformed, and reintroduced into the global supply chain. This means that businesses can use Social Plastic feedstock as raw material for their products. Some companies that partner with Plastic Bank include SC Johnson, Henkel, Advansa, and Carton Pack.

To date, Plastic Bank has stopped more than 2.8 billion plastic bottles from entering the oceans through the work of 22,000 community members and 613 recycling communities.

ECONYL

Econyl is leading the charge in innovative recycling processes. Through state-of-the-art technology, discarded clothes, rugs, old carpets, fish nets, and nylon waste are transformed into regenerated nylon, which can be used to create new products, including fashion and sportswear, apparel, carpets, and floor mats, among others.

Regenerated nylon is a high-quality fabric that is exactly the same as brand new nylon and can be used for a variety of applications across various industries, particularly in fashion, interior design, and automotive industries. Econyl is made from recycled materials, making it an environmentally friendly choice for designers, architects, manufacturers, and creatives.

Econyl's process allows them to produce raw materials from recycled nylon. And for every 10,000 tons of Econyl regenerated nylon produced, they are able to save over 70,000 barrels of crude oil and avoid greenhouse gas emissions equivalent to 65,100 tons of carbon dioxide emissions.

THE ZERO-WASTE APPROACH

Zero waste is a philosophy that encourages the redesign of resource life cycles so that all products are reused or recycled. The goal is to eliminate waste by using resources efficiently.

In 2013, a group of environmental activists, professors, industry experts, and waste professionals got together and founded the Zero Waste International Alliance (ZWIA). This global organization is open to businesses, organizations, and individuals who are working to reduce waste and achieve a zero-waste lifestyle.

ZWIA's mission is to share knowledge and best practices, and to promote the zero-waste approach, which is based on the following principles:

- Eliminating waste at its source. This can be done by designing products that are compostable and easy to recycle using sustainable production methods that mimic natural processes and closed-loops.

- Managing resources efficiently so that everything is reused and nothing is wasted. This can be done by promoting innovation in production methods to conserve resources and minimize land filling and incineration.

- Fostering collaboration with individuals and organizations with a common interest in protecting the Earth. Connecting with others creates opportunities to learn new ways to reduce plastic waste.

The first step is to audit your current waste stream. Identify what you're throwing away and why. This will help you come up with strategies to reduce or eliminate waste. You can also start small by making simple changes like bringing your own reusable bags to the grocery store or using a water bottle instead of buying bottled water. These small changes can add up to make a big impact and put you in a better position to implement a zero-waste lifestyle.

CONCLUSION: IT'S NOT TOO LATE

It's time to face the facts: plastic waste is a huge problem. The statistics are alarming and the effects of plastic pollution on our planet are devastating. We need to find viable solutions—and fast!

Let's be real here. Recycling alone is not enough. Saving the planet from plastic pollution requires a multifaceted approach that includes reducing our reliance on plastics, recycling what we can, and cleaning up our oceans—but most importantly, stopping the problem at the source. This means finding ways to reduce the amount of plastic that we produce, use, and throw away.

Plastic pollution is also a problem for the brands associated with it. These brands need to take part in revolutionizing the design of disposable plastics, and they need to do it now.

The fact is that disposable plastics are not going away anytime soon. They're too convenient, and they're too cheap. But that doesn't mean that we can't make them more environmentally friendly. We need to find ways to make them recyclable, reusable, compostable, and biodegradable so that they don't end up in our oceans and landfills. If the brands involved in this study don't want to be seen as contributing to the problem, they need to step up and take action and be part of the solution.

The particles of plastic that we can see are just the tip of the iceberg—much of the plastic in our oceans is unseen; broken down into tiny pieces that are difficult to clean up and pose a serious threat to animal and human health.

There are many things that each of us can do to help reduce the amount of plastic pollution in our world. We can refuse single-use plastics like straws, bags, and utensils; we can recycle what we use; and we can support companies and organizations who are working to reduce plastic waste.

To protect ourselves from the hidden dangers of plastic, it will take commitment, political will, and collaborative effort from governments, businesses, consumers, and non-profit organizations to make significant progress in solving the plastic pollution crisis. Plastic pollution has already caused extensive damage to our planet and cost taxpayers millions of dollars in cleanup costs. The environmental, social, economic, and health consequences of plastic pollution could get much worse if we do not act now.

Printed in Great Britain
by Amazon

15609157R00047